PENGUIN BOOKS

THE BRAVE

Rachna Bisht Rawat is a journalist, writer, mom to a precocious 12-year-old, and gypsy wife to an Army officer whose work has taken the Rawats to some of the quirkiest places in India. You can reach her at www.rachnabisht.com.

Rachna is a 2005 Harry Brittain fellow and winner of the 2006 Commonwealth Press Quarterly's Rolls Royce Award. Her first story, 'Munni Mausi', was Highly Commended in the 2008–09 Commonwealth Short Story Competition. This is her first book.

THE
BRAVE

RACHNA BISHT RAWAT

PARAM VIR
CHAKRA STORIES

PENGUIN BOOKS

PENGUIN BOOKS

Published by the Penguin Group

Penguin Books India Pvt. Ltd, 7th Floor, Infinity Tower C, DLF Cyber City, Gurgaon 122 002, Haryana, India

Penguin Group (USA) Inc., 375 Hudson Street, New York, New York 10014, USA

Penguin Group (Canada), 90 Eglinton Avenue East, Suite 700, Toronto, Ontario, M4P 2Y3, Canada

Penguin Books Ltd, 80 Strand, London WC2R 0RL, England

Penguin Ireland, 25 St Stephen's Green, Dublin 2, Ireland (a division of Penguin Books Ltd)

Penguin Group (Australia), 707 Collins Street, Melbourne, Victoria 3008, Australia

Penguin Group (NZ), 67 Apollo Drive, Rosedale, Auckland 0632, New Zealand

Penguin Books (South Africa) (Pty) Ltd, Block D, Rosebank Office Park, 181 Jan Smuts Avenue, Parktown North, Johannesburg 2193, South Africa

Penguin Books Ltd, Registered Offices: 80 Strand, London WC2R 0RL, England

First published by Penguin Books India 2014

10 9 8 7 6 5

The views and opinions expressed in this book are the author's own and the facts are as reported by her which have been verified to the extent possible, and the publishers are not in any way liable for the same.

ISBN 9780143422358

Typeset in Adobe Garamond by R. Ajith Kumar, New Delhi
Printed at Replika Press Pvt. Ltd, India

A PENGUIN RANDOM HOUSE COMPANY

For all those brave soldiers whose sacrifices went unrecognized—you were as brave as the ones we honoured

Contents

Introduction

Lest we forget

The Army has given me nearly all the men I love right from my father, who is a proud paratrooper, and my brother, also a paratrooper, to my husband, who is an engineer. And though Saransh, my 12-year-old son, wants to be a WWF wrestler as of now, there will be no one prouder than my husband and I if he does decide to join the Army.

Friends, family, cousins—these men in olive green have been around me for a lifetime, walking all over my carpet and my heart, with their dirty DMS boots, drinking Old Monk rum till kingdom come, driving me insane with their unpredictable lives, and melting me completely with a salute and a smile. And I can't thank the Army enough for giving them to me, well-groomed and spit-shined. Gallant and charming, proud yet humble, uncomfortably out of place in a materialistic world but continuing to live their lives with dignity in the most trying times, because that's the only way they've been taught. *The Brave* is for them all.

This story began one evening when I was walking down

the Mall in Ferozepur, the last cantonment on the Indo-Pak border, where kids raced bicycles and red poppies bloomed by the roadside. Looking up, I caught the eye of Company Havildar Major Abdul Hamid, PVC, of 4 Grenadiers, who was killed in 1965 while blowing up a Pakistani Patton tank from his RCL gun in the Khemkaran sector. He was watching me from a laminated poster on the roadside. I had been offered my first book contract and was a little giddy with happiness. Looking up, I declared: 'I am going to write your story, Abdul Hamid.'

Abdul Hamid did not respond but Lieutenant Colonel Manoj Rawat, my husband, who was walking by my side, smiled and stepped off the sidewalk and broke into a jog, gesturing to me to meet him end of the road when I was done. It took me a year, but I met him there.

This book signifies the end of the road that took me past fields of yellow mustard and golden wheat ripening in the sun, as I went looking for retired soldiers who had returned from wars that had claimed their comrades. I sat with them on cots pulled in the shade and shared with them their thoughts and their food. This road took me beyond the Sela Pass in Tawang, where an entire lake freezes over in the winter, to Bumla, where Subedar Joginder Singh fought with a bayonet when he ran out of bullets in the 1962 War, where soldiers lacked everything except courage. It took me to Kangra in Himachal, where fragrant white roses bloomed and the snow-covered Dhauladhar ranges accompanied me all the way to Captain Vikram Batra's house, where his father sat draped in a pashmina shawl. It took me to Sirijap in Ladakh, where Major Dhan Singh Thapa sliced necks off with his khukri;

and it took me all the way to freezing Rezang La in Chushul, where 13 Kumaon's Major Shaitan Singh and his men (113 in all) were brutally massacred because they were outnumbered completely—they died following the orders: *You will fight till the last man and the last bullet.*

When 13 Kumaon sent me a list of Rezang La martyrs, it ran into three pages on my laptop and made my eyes wet. I met two Rezang La survivors, both 73 now. They recounted how a dying Maj Shaitan, his stomach slashed open, ordered them to leave him behind since their staying would only lessen their chances of survival.

I'm sharing these stories with you to celebrate the sacrifices these men in uniform made. This book is based on interviews with families and comrades of dead soldiers—and if there are any discrepancies between the versions of different people it is because incidents were looked at from different perspectives, clouded by pain and the haze of time.

It was not an easy book to write and I give it to you as a tribute to all the brave soldiers who died fighting for us, and to their families who have lived with loss all their lives and yet been generous enough to share with me what they still have—memories of these dead heroes.

THE INDO-PAK WAR OF
1947–48

S oon after Independence and the painful partition of British India, India and Pakistan fought their first war over the princely state of Jammu and Kashmir.

In June 1947, when Partition was announced, the 600 princely states that existed then were given the choice to accede to either India or Pakistan, or remain independent. Most rulers agreed to merge with the country closer to them, while a few chose to remain independent. Maharaja Hari Singh of Jammu and Kashmir decided to avoid accession to either country. He preferred to enter into a Standstill Arrangement, which guaranteed that existing administrative arrangements would continue to be honoured until a new agreement was made. An appeal was made to both countries to not arm twist the state into taking a quick decision but to allow a people's verdict. Pakistan (which felt that since a majority of Kashmir's population was Muslim, it should be a part of Pakistan) signed the agreement but was not ready to wait.

In a crafty bid to take over Jammu and Kashmir, it started infiltrating the hill state just a few months after Independence, with a force of Pathan tribesmen, ex-soldiers and deserters from the state forces intermingled with Pakistan Army regulars. The men were well supplied with rations, arms, vehicles and medical supplies and promised extensive looting. In October 1947, the raiders started attacking the border villages and creating a deadly atmosphere of plunder, loot and rape. They did not distinguish between Hindus and Muslims; they picked up women, took them back forcibly with them, and left hundreds dead in the villages they went through.

Initially, the raiders were fought back by the state military. But realizing that the attacking lashkars were proving too strong for them, Maharaja Hari Singh requested India's help. Prime Minister Jawaharlal Nehru made a shrewd diplomatic move by offering help subject to Kashmir signing the Instrument of Accession to the Union of India. That was the only way the Indian Army could enter Jammu and Kashmir legally.

After Maharaja Hari Singh signed the document, Indian troops were sent to defend Kashmir and drive out the raiders. India had to airlift troops and equipment to Srinagar. A bloody conflict resulted. The raiders were chased out of Kashmir to beyond Baramulla and Uri and these towns were captured back. Jhanger, Rajauri, Tithwal, Kargil were other places that were recaptured by the Indian forces. The Zoji La Pass was taken over with the use of tanks, which could not have been imagined at that height, and even Dras was won.

Nehru finally asked the UN to intervene and after protracted negotiations a formal ceasefire was declared in January 1949. According to the terms of the ceasefire, Pakistan had to withdraw its forces, both regular and irregular, while allowing India to retain a minimum military strength in J&K to ensure the prevalence of peace, law and order.

Pakistan took over about two-fifth of Kashmir while India wrested control of the rest of Kashmir, which included the most fertile and prosperous regions.

Army units that participated in the action and fought bravely were awarded a total of 11 battle honours and one theatre honour. These included: Gurais, Kargil, Naushera, Srinagar, Punj, Tithwal, Rajouri and Zoji La.

It is believed that both India and Pakistan lost about 1500 men each in the war. The Indian Army fought bravely and the list of gallantry awards ran long. For their supreme acts of bravery, cold courage and devotion to duty, five soldiers were decorated with the Param Vir Chakra, independent India's highest gallantry award. Major Somnath Sharma, Naik Yadunath Singh and Company Havildar Major Piru Singh Shekhawat died fighting and were given the award posthumously, while Lance Naik Karam Singh and Second Lieutenant Rama Raghoba Rane lived to wear the medal on their chests.

Somnath Sharma

Fifteen minutes early for my appointment with Lieutenant General (retd) Surindra Nath Sharma, former engineer-in-chief of the Indian Army and younger brother of late Major Somnath Sharma, I settle down to wait in the lobby of his tastefully done up house in Defence Colony, New Delhi. The slim and remarkably fit 90-year-old Sherwoodian walks in almost immediately. He dazzles me with his memory, his firm grip on names and dates, his British accent, his delightful wit and his old-world courtesy that includes holding doors open and walking me down to my car when the interview is done.

When he recounts tales of his brother's bravery, there is pride in his voice; when he speaks about how the schoolboy Somi would march the kids in the neighbourhood up and down, he smiles nostalgically. And when he tells me about Somi's infatuation with a very young girl when he last came to meet the family in Rawalpindi in 1947, he chuckles like a schoolboy, refusing outright to tell me more.

'We don't discuss ladies,' he says gallantly. I am disarmed with his charm, but what impresses me most is the lucid manner in which he recounts the Battle of Badgam and makes Somnath Sharma and the '47 war with Pakistan come alive in front of my eyes.

––––––––

Badgam, Jammu and Kashmir
3 November 1947

Resting his plastered left arm on the edge of the trench, Maj Somnath Sharma raises his head and squints at the sun; it has moved west but there are still a few hours of daylight left. He has to move his company soon and if they make good time, they can be back at the Srinagar airfield by night. It has been a tense and gruelling morning, but now he is feeling quite relaxed.

At first light that day, a fighting patrol comprising A and D Companies of 4 Kumaon (under Somi) and one company of 1 Para Kumaon (under Captain Ronald Wood) had been sent to Badgam after intelligence reports had warned that a 1000-strong lashkar of Pathans, led by Pakistan Army regulars, was heading towards Srinagar. Their aim, the reports had said, was to take over Srinagar airfield and thus handicap the Army by cutting off their supplies. The fighting patrol's job had been to search for the raiders and engage them at Badgam, a small village three to four miles from the Srinagar airfield.

Early morning, Sharma had reported that his company was

positioned on a hillock west of the village and that they had dug trenches there. 1 Para Kumaon had established themselves south-east of the village and had reported that the village was quiet and peaceful. Sharma had also reported that the villagers had been going about their chores quietly though they looked scared. He has also noticed that some of them were clustered in a nala where they seemed to be taking shelter. Since Badgam appeared peaceful, 1 Para Kumaon was ordered to 'circle east and search; and then return to the airfield after making contact with 1 Punjab'. They did so, and were back in Srinagar by 1 p.m.

Since Badgam is quiet, Sharma is also ordered to start pulling his companies out. At 2 p.m. he reports that A Company, which had been ordered to circle to the west, had done so and was also on its way to the airfield. Somi plans to keep D Company in Badgam till late evening and then withdraw to the air field. His decision is supported by Brig. L.P. Sen, DSO. The two know each other well from battles in the Arakan in 1944–45. The soldiers are just biding time since there are only a few hours to go.

The general stops for a breather and a sip of the lemonade that has appeared by our sides and then shakes his head gravely. 'The people Somi had mistaken for villagers in the nala were in fact Pathans dressed as Kashmiri locals with weapons hidden under their loose chogas,' he grimaces.

The lashkar was arriving in Badgam in bits and pieces to conceal their movement and it was led by a Pakistani major, who was hatching a crafty plan even as he watched the soldiers of the Indian Army patrolling the village. He had asked his men to mix with the locals and wait for the rest of the Pathans, who were quietly making their way to Badgam after slowly trooping in through the gap between the ranges at Gulmarg. He planned to attack Badgam when they reached a count of around 1000 men and then advance to the Srinagar airfield. Pakistan's plan was to attack the airfield, cut off the Army's access and then takeover Jammu and Kashmir.

'It was a great plan,' the general acknowledges grudgingly.

Around 2 p.m., well after A Company left Badgam, the villagers grouped in the nala began to disperse. While Sharma and his men thought they were returning to their homes, they were quietly positioning themselves around D Company. The Pakistani major had decided not to wait beyond afternoon and as soon as he had about 700 men, he launched his attack. Sharma and his company, consisting of about 90 men, were the only ones left to fight the raiders. They were outnumbered seven to one.

———

Wrinkling his forehead in an effort to remember, Lt Gen Sharma says it was around 2.30 p.m. that Somi and his men were taken by surprise when gunfire started coming at them from the village. Soon, they were receiving machine-gun fire as well. Somi reported to his brigade commander that his position was under attack. He added that he was apprehensive about returning fire in the direction of the village because he could hurt innocent people, including women and children. By then, the raiders had started coming up in large numbers from a depression in the west.

'There were hundreds of them, and they started targeting Somi's company with mortar and automatic fire,' says Lt Gen Sharma. 'Since the Pathans were not trained soldiers, every 100 men were commanded by a Viceroy's Commissioned Officer (VCO) while every 10 men had a regular Pakistani Army soldier with them who inspired them to fight. '

Lt Gen Sharma says he heard from soldiers of 4 Kumaon who returned alive from the battle how Somi encouraged his men to retaliate and, completely unmindful of his own safety, rushed from one trench to another urging them to fight back bravely. Such was the grit and determination of the men that the first few attacks, which came from different directions, were successfully repulsed.

The Pathans, however, drew strength from sheer numbers and began to increase the pressure. Soon they had surrounded D Company from three sides and started climbing up the hillock where the trenches were. They came in hordes, brandishing automatics and shouting 'Allah ho Akbar!'

Somi knew he was outnumbered. He called the brigade commander and asked for ammunition and reinforcements. He was told that 1 Punjab was being sent for their support but Somi realized they would take time to get there since they had to move in battle formation. He also understood how important it was to hold back the enemy till reinforcements could be sent to close the gap leading to Srinagar. If that was not done, the raiders could advance right up to the airfield and take over Srinagar.

Somi decided to hold back tenaciously and urged his men to fight to the last. It is to their credit that they did, despite the fact that they were completely outnumbered and their .303

rifles were no match for the enemy's medium machine guns.

'Somi knew his company would not be able to hold out for long but he did not let his men lose confidence. With complete disregard for his own safety, he rushed across the open ground in full view of the enemy and went about encouraging his men. When the heavy casualties started affecting the men manning the light machine guns, Somi himself went around, using his good hand—his left arm was in plaster—to fill magazines and hand these over to the light machine gunners. He would tell them when and where to fire.

"Idhar maro, udhar maro," he would say, and the battle raged for almost five hours,' the general tells me. 'That was precious time for the Indian Army, since the raiders were being delayed and they were getting time to plug the gaps as they built up strength with Indian Air Force planes flying in more troops.'

Eventually, the men started running out of ammunition. When Somi informed brigade headquarters (HQ) about this, he was asked to pull back. He refused outright. 'The enemy is only 50 yards from us. We are heavily outnumbered. We are under devastating fire. I shall not withdraw an inch but will fight to the last man and the last round,' was his last message to the HQ.

Just a few minutes later, while he was crouched in a trench next to the Bren gunner, helping him load the gun, a mortar shell landed on the open ammunition box next to them. An eardrum-shattering blast rent the air. 'It blew up Somi, his sahayak (an officer's helper or man Friday who looks after his uniform and turnout), the machine gunner and a JCO, who was standing nearby,' recounts Lt Gen Sharma, his voice gentle.

For Somi, who had insisted upon leading his company to Kashmir despite having his arm in plaster, it was all over. But it is considered a credit to his leadership that the men under his command kept his word. The non-commissioned officers (NCOs) of the company decided to fight on, and they managed to hold back the raiders for another hour even after Somi had died.

In fact, as the ammunition became desperately short, another hero emerged. Lt Gen Sharma talks with great respect about Lance Naik Balwant Singh of D Company, who took a brave initiative when most of the soldiers were left with just one round or two. 'He asked them to collect whatever rounds were left with them and hand those over to him. He then loaded his gun with these two or three magazines and told the rest of the men to retreat while he held up the enemy. "There is no point in everybody dying," he said. "I will hold them back for the few minutes you need to disappear into the fields."

'So he and three others stayed back to battle the raiders while the rest left the hillock from the back. Shooting the last of their rounds, these four bravehearts got out of their trenches and charged at the enemy. They were killed but they helped their comrades survive,' recalls the general.

Overall, the brave action of D Company resulted in the raiders being delayed by close to six hours by which time the Indian Army had managed to get into position and block the enemy advance to Srinagar airfield. As aircrafts continued to fly in with more and more soldiers, the airfield defence had become strong enough to stop any attack.

On the morning of 5 November, Badgam was counter-attacked by the Indian Army and captured. The bodies of

300 raiders were counted, which proved just how ruthless the fight had been. The retaliatory fire had been so harsh that the Pathans had not been able to pick up their dead. Since they were not trained soldiers, they were not used to losing men in such a big way. The big losses broke their resolve and they started pulling back. When the Army took over Badgam, they found the Pakistanis retreating. 'When a man's will is broken, he cannot fight,' says Lt Gen Sharma.

In the battle of Badgam, 4 Kumaon lost Maj Somnath Sharma, Subedar Prem Singh Mehta and 20 other ranks. Twenty-six people were wounded in the operation. For his gallantry, tenacious defence and exemplary leadership that inspired his men to fight the enemy, in spite of being outnumbered seven to one, Maj Somnath Sharma was awarded the Param Vir Chakra (PVC) posthumously. It was the first PVC of independent India.

———

We have come to the end of the interview and, as I switch off my Dictaphone, the general stands before a beautiful oil painting of his brother, which hangs on the wall. The late Maj Somnath Sharma of D Company, 4 Kumaon, is standing in his uniform, ribbons on his chest. He looks handsome and proud.

Lt Gen Sharma turns away with a distant look in his eyes. 'Somi died. He was not there to die, he was there to kill. A job had to be done. It was his job and he did it,' he says. There is steel in his voice.

Somi doesn't answer. A half smile plays on his lips.

Maj Somnath Sharma was born on 31 January 1923, in Jammu. His father, Amarnath Sharma, was a medical corps officer, who rose to the rank of major general. Of his two brothers, Surindra Nath, better known as Tindy in Army circles, went on to become the engineer-in-chief. The youngest, Vishwa Nath, joined the armoured corps and went on to become the Chief of Army Staff in 1988. Of his two sisters, Kamla joined the Army as a doctor and married an Army officer, who also rose to the rank of Major General; the other, Manorama, also married a brigadier in the Army.

When Tindy was four years old, his father was detailed to do a medical course in England and decided to take his wife along. Somi and Tindy, who were about one year apart, were put in Hampton Court Convent in Mussoorie. Though Somi was older, they were put in the same class and made a good team. The two remained boarders there, happy to be in the same dormitory.

'We got kicked around by seniors, but Somi was my protector because he was tougher and bigger than me,' remembers Tindy. 'I was the brains behind the pair, I was very good at math, and he was more into outdoor stuff. Other than history and general knowledge, Somi was just not interested in studies.'

The deal between the brothers was that while Somi would protect Tindy from the bullies, Tindy would finish all the homework in the evening so that Somi could get up early and copy it. Both went on to study at Sherwood from where Somi, who always wanted to join the Army, applied for admission to the Prince of Wales's Royal Indian Military College (now Rashtriya Indian Military College), Dehradun.

After passing out in May 1941 he joined the Indian Military Academy (IMA) where he did exceptionally well. By then the war had started and IMA training was cut short. After about nine months of training, Somi became a commissioned officer in February 1942. He was just 19 when he joined the 8/19 Hyderabad Regiment, now 4 Kumaon, as a second lieutenant. He faced action in Arakan where one of the toughest battles of the Burma War was fought with the Japanese on the Arakan coast where three Indian battalions landed, along with one battalion of British commandos.

That was where Somi saw a wounded Kumaoni soldier sitting against a tree. He asked the man to run but when he replied that he was not be able to stand up, the tough and battle-hardy Somi carried the man on his back, right through Japanese crossfire, laughing all the way, and bringing him back to safety. The two were not shot, possibly because the Japanese respected raw courage.

Returning to India as a major and the adjutant of 4 Kumaon, Somi got busy in internal security duties in various parts of Punjab and helping the police and civil authorities in controlling civil disturbances in 1947. Many educational institutions in Delhi still talk of his great powers of organization in arranging supplies of rations and safe movement of people from one locality to another. He was made in charge of a flying squad of men with jeeps, who would assist the police in controlling civil disturbances in Delhi. His amicable but firm command instilled confidence and discipline in many difficult situations.

The same was tested when hostilities broke out in Kashmir in 1947, and India decided to send her troops to save Kashmir from the Pakistani raiders. Though Somi's left arm was in plaster due to an old wrist-fracture suffered doing gymnastics, he insisted on going with his company. As he was so keen to go, the commanding officer finally agreed and ordered him to fly in and command two companies of 4 Kumaon tasked with the protection of Srinagar airfield. There are some priceless black and white pictures of him with his arm in a cast, taken at Safdarjung Airport, where he is grinning broadly, no doubt happy with the thought of being with his men in war.

When Somi landed in Srinagar in late October, the raiders were closing in on Baramulla with Badgam on route. That was where a bloody battle would be fought and the brave young officer would bring home the first Param Vir Chakra of independent India.

Somi's life story is often quoted in books and Army messes. It is a tale of sheer courage and glory. The example set by him is recounted with a lot of respect and he is fondly remembered not only by 4 Kumaon but the entire armed forces. To ensure that young soldiers continue to be inspired by his bravery, the training ground at the Kumaon Regimental Centre in Ranikhet has been named Somnath Sharma Ground. A beautiful red brick gateway called Somnath Dwar leads to the perfectly maintained parade ground, flanked by the snow-capped Himalayas. The ground has seen the sweat and toil of thousands of young boys, new recruits of the Kumaon Regiment and the Naga Regiments, who take their first step as young soldiers here.

Sahayak:

Karam Singh

Richhmar Gali, Kashmir
13 October 1948

The Sikh soldier peering out of the trench looks worried. 'Dushman nedhe si. Assi tinn see, tey chautha tu—hun kee kariye?' (The enemy has come close. We are just three, and you are the fourth—what do we do?) he whispers to his section commander Lance Naik Karam Singh, who is standing beside him, still and ramrod straight.

Karam Singh is a handsome Sikh, more than six feet tall. A proud upturned moustache and dark beard lend him a dark, brooding appearance. He is holding a .303 rifle. His trousers are soaked with blood from the injuries he has been subjected to in the earlier gunfight. He and his men have been able to beat back the first attack from the Pakistanis, but the enemy is back with renewed vigour.

Karam Singh does not answer. His eyes are narrowed in concentration. He is watching the armed Pakistani soldiers advancing towards his outpost. There are just four men in his section and they have already been under intense shelling. All of them are bleeding from bullet as well as splintering rock hits from continuous artillery shelling by the enemy.

He looks at the gun is in his hands but he knows there are too many of them for gunfire to be effective. Besides, he is running short of ammunition and since there is continuous shelling there is no way to get more from the main company position, which is far behind. The enemy soldiers have come closer.

Karam Singh reaches into his backpack and, pulling out a grenade, bites the pin off with his teeth. Swinging his arm in a wide half-circle he flings it at them with the war cry of 'Jo bole so nihal, sat Sri Akaal'.

The physical strain of the muscle movement runs right down to his leg and he winces in pain, but he does not take his eyes off the arc of the grenade flying through the air.

It lands right in the path of the first row of advancing soldiers and a loud blast echoes through Richhmar Gali. Some of the men fall, screaming in pain; the others have lost their composure.

It is only then that Karam Singh turns to look at the tense, mud-stained faces of his tired and injured comrades and smiles. 'Jadon assi ithe jaan de dange tan saddi keemat wadh jaavegi,' (If we die fighting, we will always be remembered) he says, his voice firm. 'Sade piche bathere ne ladanwaale. Saari company sade piche hai.' (There are many who will continue the fight after we *die) With that, he rummages in his backpack for another grenade, removes the pin and tosses it at those of the enemy soldiers who are still advancing. Another deadly blast rents the air.*

———————

Lance Naik Karam Singh was commanding an Alpha Company outpost at Richhmar Gali when around 6 a.m. on 13 October 1948 his section came under a do-or-die attack from the Pakistanis. It was Id, and the Pakistanis had launched a desperate attack to win back the area they had lost to the Indian Army. Karam Singh and his men were completely outnumbered, but they refused to be cowed down by the enemy whose aim was to recapture Richhmar Gali, skirt Tithwal and move in to attack Srinagar.

The enemy soldiers were coming in wave after wave in a bid to take over the outpost of A Company of 1 Sikh. It is to their credit that Karam Singh and his men managed to hold on to their post during two fierce attacks—the first of which came at 6 a.m. and the second followed at 9.30 a.m.

The men of 1 Sikh still talk about how these two attacks could be beaten back only because of Karam Singh's courage and will to fight till the end. He is believed to have stemmed the enemy advances almost singlehandedly and wiped out two sections with his perfectly aimed grenades. But after repulsing the second attack, the brave soldier was quick to realize that he would not be able to hold on for much longer. He and his men were heavily outnumbered at one to ten; three of them had already sustained serious injuries and they were also running out of ammunition. In the intense artillery shelling and mortar fire that was coming from the enemy there was no hope of ammunition being brought to them from the main company position either. He decided to rejoin the main company, but insisted on carrying along his two badly wounded comrades.

Without a thought for his own safety or injuries, he pulled out the two wounded men with the help of the fourth soldier, who was the only one left unharmed. Putting their lives on hold, the two of them dragged the injured men through the intense enemy shelling and managed to get them back to the main company bunkers.

Around 10 a.m., the enemy launched another attack, this time on the company position. Without a thought for his grievous injuries, Karam Singh went about fighting from the frontline trenches. He held on even when the enemy mortar fire and shelling managed to destroy almost every single bunker of the platoon. Moving from bunker to bunker, he implored his tired men to continue being brave; to fight like proud Khalsa warriors. He helped in getting the wounded out and encouraged the uninjured to fight back without fear. He did not let the morale of the soldiers sag though the day when the enemy launched one attack after another.

During one of these attacks, Karam Singh was injured yet again, but he kept his faith and, despite the depleting strength of the company, continued the fight. In the next attack that came around 1 p.m., Karam Singh immortalized himself in the war records of his paltan (unit) by another exemplary act of bravery.

Fifth Pakistani attack, 1 p.m.

The Pakistani soldiers have launched a fifth attack. There has been no respite since 6 a.m. and the tiredness as well as the strain of his injury is bogging Karam Singh down. He grits his teeth to bear the pain and trains his gun on the enemy soldiers moving forward through the grenade smoke. He finds that two of them have sprinted the final few yards and are now right in front of his trench, brandishing their rifles. They are too close to be shot without hurting his own men. Without hesitating for a second, Karam Singh fixes the bayonet on to his rifle and leaps out of the trench. Lifting the bayonet in the air with a blood-curdling war cry, he shoves it right inside the chest of the Pakistani soldier in front of him. Before the shocked man can realize what has happened, the hefty Sikh has struck again. 'Ghonp nikal, ghonp nikal', Karam Singh mumbles under his breath, remembering the drill taught to him by his ustad (instructor), at the centre.

The enemy soldier lies dead before him, horror writ large in his open eyes. Pulling the bayonet out of his body, Karam Singh pulls it back as far as his arms can go and in a split second brings it forward again with force, pushing it into the stomach of the next man, who is trying to shoot. A fountain of red springs forth as the lethal blade cuts into the man's skin and intestines, making him double up and collapse in pain and terror. Karam Singh pulls his bayonet out, and lifting his arm right over his head, pushes it into the fallen man once again relieving him of all pain forever. He jumps back into the trench before his comrades can even fathom what has happened.

Shocked by this savage attack and the coldblooded killings by the hefty Sikh warrior, the enemy soldiers retreat one more time. They do not give up though and keep returning despite being beaten back each time by the strong defence put up by the company.

It is 7 p.m. when the enemy's will is finally broken and they give up. By then, they have launched eight attacks on Karam Singh's company, all of which had been repulsed by the Sikhs. They have fired 3,000 shells, which have taken a heavy toll and destroyed almost all the A Company bunkers but have not been able to break the spirit of the men. 1 Sikh lose 10 men and have 37 wounded during the battle, which is later described by division commander Major General K.S. Thimayya, DSO as a 'uniquely magnificent fight'. Lance Naik Karam Singh MM is awarded the Param Vir Chakra (PVC) for his devotion to duty and bravery beyond comparison. He is the first soldier to receive it live.

Not only did Karam Singh survive his injuries; he even marched up to India's first President, Dr Rajendra Prasad, to receive his PVC.

This was his second gallantry award. He had been awarded the Military Medal for his bravery in Burma while he was fighting under the British. He was among the five persons chosen by Prime Minister Jawaharlal Nehru to hoist the National Flag on 15 August 1947. He lived on to 77 years of age, rose to the rank of Honorary Captain in his beloved battalion and died peacefully at home in 1993.

Karam Singh is fondly remembered by his regiment as the war hero who not only inspired his men to fight and kill, but also helped them retain their confidence despite being grossly outnumbered in the battle of Richhmar Gali.

———

Most of what I learnt about Karam came from Subedar Kala Singh, retired soldier from 1 Sikh, who was Lance Nayak Karam Singh's sahayak many years back. I took a train, then a 45-km ride out of Bathinda in an Army gypsy, to visit him in his brick-lined house in Chehalanwali village.

The interview was accompanied by Kala Sahab's warm Punjab hospitality, which included endless glasses of sour lassi, rotis served with ghee and pickle, and a photo session with the entire family, which included the family goat and tractor.

Old man Kala has a twinkle in his eye when he talks of Karam Singh Saab. He served with the '48 war hero and has many memories he is keen to share.

'We all knew Saab had got a Military Medal in Burma when he was a young soldier. Though he did not talk about it all that much, he would often tell us of episodes from the battle of Richhmar Gali, when he almost singlehandedly foiled Pakistanis bid to take over Company Post. He was a man with guts,' says Kala. 'He could fight not just in war but also in peace. When he felt something was not right, he would never hesitate to say it.'

When Karam Singh was the quarter master havaldar of 1 Sikh, Kala was appointed his helper. Besides routine jobs, Kala's work involved reading and writing documents on behalf of Karam. 'Saab had never gone to school. He could barely write his own name, so I would help him make ration cards, condemnation boards, etc.,' he says.

Kala likes to recount an incident that brings out how fearless and forthright Karam Singh was. 'In the early 60s, Karam Singh was in the Sikh Regimental Centre at Meerut. He was asked to buy sugar for the soldiers from a local mill and was doing that when someone brought to his notice that the sacks of sugar were being soaked in water to increase their weight. A furious Karam told the mill that he would not accept any wet sacks. The mill owner, who was a corrupt but well-connected man, had an argument with Karam. When Karam stuck to his stand the mill owner pushed him physically and threatened him saying he had connections in Delhi.

The hot-headed Karam had reached the end of his patience. He beat up the mill owner. The case was reported and since the mill owner had connections in high places, Karam was dismissed from service as punishment for manhandling a civilian.

Not one to take injustice lying down, Karam went to Delhi with his war medals and sought an interview with the President. It was granted. When he explained to the President what had transpired, he was immediately reinstated in service.

The jawans were thrilled with his victory. Karam had been proved a hero in their eyes once again. 'Ek kahawat hai jee, karela—woh bhi neem chada,' (A bitter gourd, that too one that grows on neem) chuckles Kala Singh, rubbing a hand over his white beard. 'Ek toh pehle hi kadwa, upar se neem ke ped pe chad ke baitha hua. Aisa tha Karam Singh Saab. Ek toh sardar tha upar se uske pas award tha!' (His fearlessness was compounded by his forthrightness. That was our Karam Singh Sahib—for one he was a sardar and then he had his awards!)

Karam Singh was born on 15 September 1915, while World War I was being fought. The son of Sardar Uttam Singh, a well-off farmer in Sehna village, near Sangrur in Punjab, Karam grew up tending to the fields and playing kabaddi with the boys. He never went to school and could not write much beyond his own name.

This did not stop him from rising in the forces; he became the quarter master havaldar of his battalion. He was sharp and intelligent, which made up for his lack of writing ability.

He was enrolled in the Army on 15 September 1941 and was sent to 1 Sikh, which was posted in the then North-East Frontier Agency. He was a good sportsman, excelling at high jump and pole vault, and was recognized in his company as a very brave man right from when he was a young soldier.

Much of his reputation came from the Military Medal that he won for his bravery during the Burma war in 1944. He thus became a hero for his battalion at a very young age. Most of the time while he was in the battalion, he stayed posted in Alpha Company, which was where he got both his gallantry awards.

Karam Singh married Gurdial Kaur in the early 1950s. The couple had two children—a son and a daughter. The son studied till class 10 and then took to farming while the daughter got married.

Karam holds the distinction of being the first living soldier to wear a PVC on his chest.

Rama Raghoba Rane

Jammu and Kashmir
April 1948

Rama Raghoba Rane is on his stomach and crawling under a Stuart tank that is slowly making its way across a minefield. He is trying to do it at a pace that matches the speed of the tank that is moving above him. His leg, badly slashed from exploding mortar, hurts with any movement but he ignores the pain, concentrating instead on the massive wheels that are turning with a deep rumble that is reverberating in his ears. Rane holds in both his hands thick ropes that are attached to the tank. He is using them as a signal for the tank to stop or move. Each time he spots a mine ahead, he pulls the rope in his right hand and the tank stops. After he has cleared the mine, he pulls the rope in his left hand and the tank starts moving again.

The armoured vehicles are part of a plan to attack Rajouri and stop the Pakistani raiders, who are intent on carnage, rape and loot. Since every second means a difference between life and death for innocent locals, speed is of the essence and the Indian Army must get there as fast as it can.

Rane has devised this method of moving in the minefield under cover of a tank since the area is under constant enemy machine gunfire and his mine-clearing section is not able to work otherwise.

He spots a telltale, circular depression that means there is an anti-tank mine lying underneath. He tugs on the rope in his right hand. Above him the tank grinds to a stop. Using the fingers of both his mud-streaked, calloused hands, Rane scrapes the stones and rubble from around the mine. He then gently removes the cover and reaches in to deactivate the fuse. Putting the lid back on again, he closes his eyes for a fraction of a second and heaves a sigh of relief. He then tugs the rope in his left hand and starts crawling again.

———

Eighty-nine-year-old Colonel J.P. Chopra, Vir Chakra, sits in his bungalow in Sector 31, Noida, with Pepper and Cookie, his two spitzes scampering around him. 'Cookie leave,' he says brusquely, and Cookie stops wagging her tail and squeezes herself under the sofa. Pepper slinks out of the door and hides behind the curtain, waiting for a chance to join the conversation again.

It has been more than sixty-five years since the Colonel and Rane were together in the same company, but the colonel's memory of the time is vivid. They were from the Engineers unit, and their job was to clear mines, make roads where there were none, and help the Army attack the Pakistani raiders in Kashmir. 'It was late 1947, war clouds were looming, and Pakistan was attacking Kashmir from two directions—from the Srinagar airfield and also from the Jammu side where they were coming on to the Akhnoor–Naushera axis,' he recalls.

The Indian Army had to pull back from Jhangar and retreat to Naushera. Then they were ordered to go back and attack Jhangar. While 2nd Lt Chopra and a section of 11 people were tasked with clearing the path towards Jhangar, Rane was with two sections (22 men), trying to make a road for the tanks to attack Rajouri.

The men, would cross nalas that would swell from six inches of water to ten feet depths if it rained. They would work with little food and rest, often subsisting on dry shakarparas to get the work done as fast as they could. Persisting even as a tank was blown up when it went over a mine, they lost count of days and dates as they cleared the dead and helped injured soldiers, laying out roads, removing obstacles and clearing mines so that the Army could reach Rajouri and stop the carnage the Pakistani raiders were indulging in.

To Rane goes the credit of getting the Army to Rajouri and thus saving many innocent lives.

Advance to Rajouri

It is 6 a.m. on a sunny April day when Rama Raghoba Rane and his section are put on mine-clearing duty starting from Nadpur South Fort area, near Naushera. Their task is to create a safe passage for tanks so that they can move from Naushera to

Rajouri, where the raiders are attacking the civilian population.

After the recapture of Jhangar, the Pakistani army flees, but not before completely destroying the national highway from Rajouri to Punj. With no other way to reach Rajouri the Indian troops are ordered to create their own route till Chingas, which is an old Mughal passage to Kashmir. 2nd Lt Rane and his section of 37 Assault Field Company are attached to 4 Dogra, which starts the advance to Rajouri on 8 April 1948, with an attack on Barwali ridge, 11 km north of Naushera. They drive out the enemy and capture Barwali ridge by 4.30 p.m. but cannot go beyond because not only is the area hilly, there are also massive road blocks and minefields on the road.

This is when Rane and his small team of Sappers are pressed into action. They start clearing the road blocks, but it gets dark soon and they are surprised by enemy fire. The Pakistanis have returned and are launching mortar bursts at the men trying to clear the road. In a stroke of bad luck, Rane loses four of his men. Sappers Abaji More and Raghunath More are killed; Sappers Sitaram Sutar and Keshav Ambre are badly wounded and later die in hospital, while a splinter hits Lance Naik M.K. Jadhav in the spine, paralysing him for life. Rane also gets a deep cut from a splinter that slashes his thigh but he refuses to be evacuated despite the heavy bleeding from his leg and asks only for first aid.

The bulldozer operator does not hear the enemy fire since his own dozer is making so much noise and has to be pulled out and evacuated. Though the Pakistanis are chased off again, plans to clear the road block at night are dropped.

Rane returns at dawn the next day to start clearing the landslide again. By 10 a.m., he has managed to clear the road block and the tanks move ahead. It soon run into another landslide that is again cleared by Rane by 3 p.m. The procedure continues, with Rane hitching a ride on the tanks; each time there is a hindrance in the path, he quickly dismounts along with his men and they work on clearing the track. They encounter fallen trees that have to be blown up, a culvert that has been damaged so badly that a new path has to be made and continuous enemy fire that has to be dodged. This continues till dusk when the tanks are halted and the men quickly dig trenches for themselves and take cover for the night.

Around 4.45 a.m. the next day Rane is back on the job. Despite great risk to his life, he continues to clear road blocks and minefields, helping the tanks move ahead. Slowly and steadily, they make a path for the advancing troop of tanks, and reach Chingas at 2 p.m.

Rane keeps working till 9 p.m. to open the road completely. Finally, at 11 a.m. the next day, the road is thrown open to all vehicles but the men soon discover that the road from Chingas has even worse road blocks. Since reports of the massacres in Rajouri are reaching the Army, a decision is taken for the rest of Rane's unit to work at clearing the road from Chingas, while he and his platoon make a path for the tanks along the bed of the river Tawi all the way to Rajouri.

The men get to work again, blowing up the big boulders along the riverside. The river follows an undulating course and often the tanks have to get in and out of water. Sometimes, they get stuck and have to be pulled out. On 11 April, they halt again and finally, on 12 April at 6 p.m., the tanks reach Rajouri. Rane has worked without any rest all these days and it is a miracle that he has managed to get the men of 1 Kumaon and the tanks there.

Once the men reach Rajouri, they find it is a ghost town. They cross two blood-soaked pits of bodies, including those of women and children who have been massacred by the raiders. The arrival of the Army ends the violence and soon refugees start returning to their villages. The engineers are awarded the battle honour of Rajouri and Rane the Param Vir Chakra for his devotion to duty, courage and gallantry.

———

Major Rama Raghoba Rane's act of exemplary courage would be remembered for a long time by the regiment, as also by the woman who loved him most. The memory of his courage is one of the first things Mrs Rajeshwari Rane, his widow, shares with me when I ask her about her husband, one of the rare men who wore a PVC alive.

The other indelible memory she has of him is of the time they first saw each other. He was the chief guest at her school, the brave officer being felicitated for the PVC he had received. She was a student of class 12, on stage singing a welcome song.

———

Love at first sight

There was much excitement in Shivaji High School, Sadashivgarh, Karwar taluka, that day. 2nd Lt Rama Raghoba Rane was being felicitated for winning the highest gallantry award of the country. The programme began with a chorus of girls singing a swagat geet. Leela was one of the singers and she gave it her best.

As an embarrassed Rane looked on, his eyes fell upon a beautiful girl in a sari. She was singing sweetly, with all her heart, looking with awe at him. The moment he saw her, he felt she was the one he wanted to spend the rest of his life with and lost no time in expressing this desire to her family.

Leela was only 19 then. Rane was a national hero and though there was an age difference of more than 15 years between the two of them, her family was only too happy to accept him as their son-in-law. On 3 February 1955, the two got married.

Seventy-eight years old now, Mrs Rane sits in her Pune house and smiles gently at the memory of her 19-year-old self and the bold and brave Army officer who fell in love with her. 'He extended his leave and left only after we had got married. Before that he asked me if he could change my name to Rajeshwari. He told me that during the PVC felicitations that were happening for him around the country he had once been invited to a maharaja's palace and there he had seen the maharani whose name was Rajeshwari. She was really beautiful and had impressed him thoroughly.

'When he came back home he had prayed to god that he should also get a girl who was as beautiful as she was. When he saw me for the first time, I reminded him of her and he felt I was the one for him. "Kya aapko Rajeshwari naam pasand hai?" (Do you like the name Rajeshwari?) he had asked and I had said yes. Hum sadharan log the. Unhone mujhe maharani ka darja de diya,' (We were ordinary folk. He elevated me to a queen) she says shyly.

She recounts many stories of his brave and fearless temperament, some of which she heard from him or his colleagues, others that happened in front of her eyes in the years that they lived together. She tells me how when he was serving in Kashmir, a girl once fell into a well; he jumped in without a thought for his own safety and brought her out.

Another time, when they had been married just a few years, he had taken her for a movie at Bhanuvilas Hall in Pune. A fight had broken out in the crowd waiting outside the hall and it had taken a very violent turn. When things started getting uncontrollable, Rane leaped into the fighting mob and brought it under control by shouting at the crowd. Again, he did not think about his own safety even as his extremely worried young wife watched on quietly.

Then, in 1962, while Rane was posted in Calcutta, Hindu–Muslim riots broke out. Detailed to contain the riots, Rane would walk often right inside deeply communal mohallas, while Rajeshwari would spend her time next to the phone, sick with fear, waiting for calls that could tell her if her husband was safe.

Rama Raghoba Rane came from a martial race, the Ranes, who had migrated to south India. He belonged to the Konkan Kshatriya Maratha community of Karwar. Bravery seemed to have been in his genes. He served in the Army for 21 years and had the distinction of getting five Mentioned-in-Despatches for his bravery and enterprise. Not only did he earn a name for himself during the trouble with Pakistan in 1947–48, he was also known for his acts of bravery during his tenure in Burma during World War II. He is said to have shot down an enemy plane with his medium machine gun.

Rane was born in Chendia village, in Karnataka, on 26 June 1918. His father was a head constable of police. He studied in the district schools, moving frequently with his father because of his transfers. He was interested in sports, outdoor activities and adventure right from when he was a small boy.

When World War II broke out, 22-year-old Rane decided to join the Army and was recruited into the Bombay Sappers in July 1940. During the passing-out parade, he stood very high in the order of merit and was presented with the Commandant's Cane for best recruit.

He remained in 37 Field Company till August 1950 after which he was posted to the Bombay Engineer Group centre. He got his PVC in 1951. In July 1954, he was awarded the Chief of Army Staff's Commendation Card for devotion to duty for his work during the Maha Prabhu Mela in Kashmir.

Rane went on to command a bomb-disposal platoon and retired as a Major on 25 June 1968. But his love for the Army did not let him leave and he sought re-employment; he continued to wear the uniform till April 1971.

After retirement, he settled down in Pune. He passed away at 73, in 1994, after undergoing an operation where the doctors were not able to stop his bleeding. He is survived by his wife Mrs Rajeshwari Rane, who continues to live in Pune.

Jadunath Singh

Tain Dhar, Kashmir
6 February 1948

Dawn has not broken, but all signs indicate it is going to be a cold and grey February morning. There is frost on the grass, masking the green with translucent white fluff. A swirling mist swept in through the night and a dense fog still hangs over the slopes of Tain Dhar Ridge, where the ten men of 9 Platoon, C Company, of 1 Rajput battalion, sit guarding picket Number 2. They have just finished making tea in silence and are now, over steaming enamel mugs of the milk powder-sweetened brew, exchanging their concerns with each other in hoarse whispers, their voices still gruff from another endless, stressful night.

The orders for them had been to defend the picket, which lies on the left shoulder of the Tain Dhar range, against an enemy attack and they have been holding fort sincerely, though it has been peaceful so far. Intelligence reports have repeatedly hinted that Pakistani raiders, out to take over Kashmir, would be heading for Naushera, and Tain Dhar falls on the way, which is why the men have been placed there. Every day and every night, the soldiers waited for an attack, but there have been none, even though excessive enemy build up had been reported in the areas around.

Shivering in their trenches in the brutal cold of Kashmir that morning, the ten men do not know that today is going to be the day. Thousands of Pakistani raiders have crept up on their tiny post in the darkness of the night and are just waiting for daybreak to attack.

It is getting late and the shadows are falling when our car cruises into Beas Military Station where 4 Guards, earlier called 1 Rajput, are stationed.

Winding between tractors, cars and motorcycles driven by brightly turbaned sardars who don't give a damn about traffic rules has been painful and frankly I'm not expecting much even at the end of the journey.

It has been more than 50 years since Naik Jadunath Singh or Yadunath Singh (the records call him both names) died and so far the leads have come to nothing. All the soldiers who fought the terrible battle of Tain Dhar with Yadunath Singh are dead too. He never married, so there is no real family to speak to. I'm seriously worried about how I'll write this Param Vir Chakra account.

In sheer desperation, I visit Beas where 4 Guards are

located. The only information I have comes from the memoirs of the late Lieutenant Colonel Kishan Singh Rathore, who was a young captain during the battle of Tain Dhar. He has written: 'Since the enemy was so close there was no question of covering fire and there was only hip firing and lobbing of grenades. The attack was frontal, we were grateful that they did not attack from the sides. Had the enemy attacked us at night, they would have won within five minutes and we would have all been slaughtered. It was then that the most astonishing thing happened. The enemy blew the retreat bugle and at almost the same time Major Gurdial Singh of 3 Rajput arrived. The enemy lost over a thousand men and victory was so complete that from then on Naushera front, the enemy was keener on running than fighting.'

I learn that it took seven days for the battalion to clear the bodies that numbered in thousands. The enemy did not claim its dead. After nearly three days the stench was such that the defences could not be occupied.

A little more of what I know comes from retired Brigadier N. Bahri of 4 Grenadiers, who now lives in Noida. Brig. Bahri tells me that when he joined the battalion in 1960 and was appointed the adjutant, Naik Yadunath had already been dead for 12 years. But Subedar Major Ami Singh, who was the 9 Platoon commander during the battle of Tain Dhar, would often tell him about Yadunath. 'Ami Singh would talk vividly of the operation and would start crying each time he spoke of Yadunath Singh,' Brig. Bahri remembers.

But I still did not have Yadunath's complete story and as a last-ditch effort, I take on the nine-hour drive from Delhi to Beas that will bring me to the battalion's present location.

There, I've been told, they have an archive where old war-diaries lie preserved. They are my last hope.

Shortly after crossing the Beas River that murmurs conversationally along the mustard fields that glow a faint yellow in the moonlight, I see a big gate looming. Param Vir Paltan, 4 Guards, it proclaims proudly. Inside, we cross Broon's Bungalow (the commandant's residence, named after Major George Sackville Brown, the first commandant). I'm told that since the Indians pronounced his name Broon in those days, the nomenclature has stuck and the battalion has continued to call itself Broon ka Paltan. A smiling Mess Havaldar R.D. Tiwari waits beside a painted signboard that says Yadunath Parade Ground. He guides us to the mess, where a shining bust of Yadunath is placed.

Lieutenant Aditya Tanwar, a tall, lanky fourth-generation officer, springs forth to open and close doors for me and then escorts me to the battalion archives where framed pictures of Yadunath and the other braves of the Battle of Tain Dhar look down from a wall. In the next room are neat stacks of war diaries, with fading yellow parchment paper that have been treated at the Indian Military Academy; they are bound carefully and covered with plastic.

Aditya bends over and proudly points out the exact noting, done in pen on paper on 6 February 1948, recounting the battle where Naik Yadunath Singh got his Param Vir Chakra. He points to 23 glass jars that are neatly lined in a corner. Filled with stones and mud, they are labelled with the names of all 23 places where the battalion has fought various battles and received battle honours.

As I lean over to read—while Havaldar Pramesh (archives-in-charge for fourteen years) and Lt Tanwar discuss Yadunath's last battle in respectful whispers—I am struck by a fascinating thought. Soldiers don't die when bullets pierce their hearts and heads through their olive green shirts and woollen balaclavas. They don't die when they fall before an enemy onslaught, or even when they get buried in trenches, staining the earth with their warm crimson blood. It is only when we forget their acts of bravery that soldiers die. And, though we have killed many that way, the officers and men of 4 Guards, Param Vir Paltan, have made Yadunath immortal by remembering him every single day of their lives. He lives in their battalion parade ground, in their mess, their archives, their thoughts and their conversations. He might not be around anymore but, strangely enough, Naik Yadunath, of the dark eyes and upturned moustache, continues to stride across their mess and their unit lines as pulsating with life as you or I are. Or, as he himself was on 6 February 1948, when he commanded a section of nine men and defended Tain Dhar when thousands of raiders launched an offensive to capture Naushera and the Jammu province.

The trouble

When India became independent, Jammu and Kashmir was one princely state that refused to accede to either India or Pakistan. However, Pakistan hatched a plot to attack and take over the province, and built up a huge force of raiders. The raiders began to attack the border towns and created a terrible atmosphere of murder, mayhem, loot and rape. The maharaja of J&K approached the Indian government for help, but the Indian government told him the army could not fight outside their own country's borders. The maharaja was asked to sign the document of accession to India and as soon as he had done so, the Indian Army was sent to defend its borders.

1 Rajput was one of the chosen battalions. It had a brief stay of two months at Gurdaspur to integrate two new companies and prepare to move operations to J&K. The unit moved to Naushera by road and reached there by 8 December 1947. It came under the 50 Para Brigade and soon the companies were spread out over posts that included Pt. 2533, Area Kot, Tain Dhar, Pt. 3319 and Pt. 3754. They were given the task of defending the Jammu–Akhnoor–Naushera–Rajouri–Poonch road axis.

The men went in for heavy patrolling of the area but there were strong reports of the enemy forces building up for an attack. On the night of 5–6 February, the listening posts warned of the enemy accumulating north of Naushera. An attack could be expected, most probably at Tain Dhar, where Naik Yadunath manned a picket with very limited men and ammunition at his disposal.

---

6 February 1948

It was dawn and a weak orange sun was slowly lighting up the horizon. Looking into the distance Yadunath noticed moving specks that appeared to be coming closer. The fog was hampering his vision and he wasn't sure if it was just an illusion of the mind so he nudged the soldier standing next to him and they both watched in quiet concentration.

Yadunath had not been mistaken. The Pakistani raiders were here and, even as his eyes adjusted to the translucent haze, he noticed that they were slowly coming closer. The time for battle had come. As Yadunath's eyes darted from one speck to another, he realized that there were hundreds of them; fully armed and striding across the vegetation. A cold shiver ran down his spine. He had only nine soldiers with him. The enemy had surrounded them in numbers he couldn't even count. He and his men had only choices. To surrender or fight till the last man. He knew what he was going to do.

Even as Yadunath and his men watched from their trenches, the specks in the distance turned into the bearded, sunburnt faces of Pakistani raiders and Pathans. Guns in hand they were now emerging one after the other from the thickets and behind rocks and boulders.

The moment they were within firing distance, they started shooting, and soon the surrounding hills rang with the sound of machine-gun and mortar fire. The raiders had a mad ferocity about them. They had been promised wealth and women. Some of their comrades had already returned home with the booty and the women they had abducted after raiding border villages and the others were looking forward to the same experience. They had not expected the Indian Army to come to Kashmir's aid, but they were prepared for battle and they knew the Indian soldiers were heavily outnumbered.

Yadunath shouted to his men to take position and together the ten brave men directed their light machine guns at the first wave of attackers.

Cries of '*Allah hu Akbar*' rang out as the two warring

sections met. As soon as an enemy soldier fell dead, two more would take his place. The men came like a swarm of locusts. In hundreds. One after another. They made their way to the picket in droves, shooting continuously.

Yadunath and his men started flinging hand grenades at them but despite that some of the raiders managed to enter the trenches. Bloody hand-to-hand combat followed with clashing bayonets glistening in the morning sun. The first wave of raiders was eventually beaten back, but at a heavy cost.

Of Yadunath's force of ten, four men had been wounded. They had barely recovered when the second wave of the assault came—stronger and even more brutal. The raiders managed to get so close that Havaldar Daya Ram, the mortar NCO (non-commissioned officer), took a big chance. Putting his own life at stake, he removed the secondary charges from the tubes to fire within 35–50 yards of the unit defences.

The mortar fire became more accurate, but it was so close that there was danger of Daya Ram killing his own men. It is to his credit that the risk was overcome and great devastation caused amongst the attacking raiders.

The brave men were unfortunately completely outnumbered and almost all the soldiers of Yadunath's section had been injured. The cries of the injured men rent the air but even then those who could stand continued to hold their guns despite their injuries and fought.

Yadunath himself had received bullet injuries on his right arm and thigh. Though badly hurt, he dragged himself to his wounded Bren gunner and took over the gun. By this time the enemy had reached the walls of the post, but Yadunath and his men did not give up. One of the non-combatants, who was not even trained to fight, also picked up an enemy rifle and shot dead a few attackers. Records say that when his ammunition finished he picked up an enemy sword and charged bravely at the raiders till he was finally shot dead.

There are many such stories of bravery, but Yadunath's towered above all the others. Battered and bleeding yet completely unmindful of his own safety, he encouraged his men to fight and battled valiantly by their side. He fought so bravely and with such unflinching courage and determination that what looked like certain defeat was turned into victory. The post was saved a second time.

By now, however, all the men of the post had become casualties. Realizing this, the enemy was quick to attack again. In the third attack, Naik Yadunath Singh, now wounded and alone, rose to fight singlehandedly.

Like a warrior blessed with eternal life, he came out of the trenches, bloody and limping, gun in hand. Firing at the enemy, his injured arm dripping blood, he charged. Shocked by his mad disregard for personal safety, the surprised enemy fled in disorder.

Yadunath was still walking when a bullet came whizzing and lodged in his chest. He ignored it and continued to fire till another one whipped into his head. Eyes still open and breathing fire, Yadunath dropped to his knees and crumbled in front of No. 2 picket of Tain Dhar. His bullet-riddled body lay there with his eyes still staring at the retreating enemy soldiers. And there Naik Yadunath Singh breathed his last. He had not allowed the enemy to take over his picket.

It was discovered later that Yadunath suffered eight bullet wounds during the three waves of the attack. There were many other heroes besides him who died fighting that day. They were men who had lived up to the highest traditions of bravery and glory.

Yadunath Singh stood tall for his own sacrifice. For his gallant action in the face of the enemy, he was honoured posthumously with the Param Vir Chakra. His story has been immortalized in the battalion war records.

The war record of 6 February 1948 that I come across in the 4 Guards archives, written in ink on parched paper that feels brittle to the touch, reads: *'No. 2, 9, 7 and Kipper's post attacked simultaneously. Enemy put in about 1500 to 2000 on each piquet. Enemy launched the attack in several waves. The battle lasted for two hours. Last wave beaten back by cold steel and bayonet. Enemy retired leaving 260 bodies, 131 rifles, and over 200 swords. Total enemy casualties believed 3000 killed, 1000 wounded. Own casualties— 21 killed and 62 wounded.*

Naik Yadunath Singh was born on 21 November 1916 in Khajuri village of Shahjahanpur in Uttar Pradesh to a poor farmer called Birbal Singh Rathore. The young Yadunath was attached to his mother, Jamuna Kanwar. He was one of eight siblings—seven boys and a girl.

The family was not very well off—there were many mouths to feed—and Yadunath had no access to a good education. Till he was in class 4, he attended the village school, working in the fields or at home after school to contribute to the family.

He was noticed in the village because he became a wrestling champion and would often sort out goons who misbehaved.

He was also deeply religious and a staunch devotee of Hanuman, so much so that he took a vow to remain a bachelor for life and followed it.

When Yadunath was 25 years old, he enrolled in the Rajput Regiment on 21 November 1941 at the regimental centre, Fategarh. After he had completed his training he was sent to the 1st battalion of the Rajput Regiment. He took part in World War II, showing glimpses of leadership and gallantry even then. He was promoted to the rank of naik and appointed commander of a section of troops. His true colours showed in the battle of Tain Dhar, where he bravely battled a fierce enemy despite his men being completely outnumbered.

Yadunath's performance continues to be a great inspiration to the men of his battalion even now. Every year, Naushera Day is celebrated in 4 Guards with great solemnity and a presentation is made on the battle of Tain Dhar by the officer commanding C Company to acknowledge and remember the great act of bravery performed by Naik Yadunath Singh in 1948.

The hero lives on.

Piru Singh Shekhawat

The Battle of Darapari
18 July 1948

It is a dark-purple moonlit night. But Company Havaldar Major (CHM) Piru Singh cannot afford to look up. The route is steep and filled with loose stones; one misstep can send him plunging down into the valley, leaving a mass of broken flesh and bones.

Piru Singh's boot has just struck a rock that has gone tumbling down. For a fraction of a second, he stops to look at its deep descent. And then he looks up at the treacherous ridge he and his section from Delta Company, 6 Rajputana Rifles (Raj. Rif.), are trudging up. If he arches his neck right up, at an angle of nearly 180 degrees, he can see where the mountain ends, dark, craggy, uninviting. That is where the enemy sits and that is where he and his men are headed.

D Company has been tasked with attacking and dislodging Pakistani irregulars from Darapari in the Tithwal sector of Kashmir. It is at a height of 11,481 feet and the attacking company has been told that the enemy is sitting there watching the narrow path that winds its way up though they have probably not had enough time to dig in deep. Piru Singh takes a few deep breaths and resumes his climb; the air is starting to get colder and the long march of 30 miles all the way from Tangdhar has started telling on the spirit of the soldiers. He knows they are tired. So is he. But in war tiredness is the least of a soldier's concern.

To distract himself from the long climb ahead, Piru Singh lets his thoughts drift to nine months back. His battalion had been in Gurgaon, involved in internal security duties when orders came for them to move to Kashmir. The hill state needed to be defended from raiding Pathans and Pakistani Army regulars. The soldiers were airlifted to Srinagar on 5 November 1947. For many of them it was the first ride in an airplane and for a few moments at least the threat of war was overshadowed by the thrill of that first plane ride.

Once in Kashmir, the battalion was thrown in the midst of action and the brave men more than proved themselves in the first few months. In April 1948, they were sent to Uri and had fought back a vicious enemy attack where they inflicted major damages on the enemy. They went on to capture an enemy position on the night of 29 April for which Rifleman Dhonkal Singh was awarded a Maha Vir Chakra posthumously. He had immediately become a battalion hero. Dhonkal had guided his platoon through a thick pine forest along a ridge and had faced the brunt of enemy light-machine-gun fire. In spite of suffering a serious injury on his left shoulder, Dhonkal

Singh had crawled ahead and destroyed the enemy post by flinging a hand grenade at it. Hit by splinters in the face and chest, he had known he would not live long, and had used all his remaining strength to lob another grenade at the retreating enemy soldiers, killing them instantaneously. The post had been captured by 6 Raj. Rif., but Dhonkal Singh had succumbed to his injuries.

Piru Singh, full of respect for his brave comrade, does not know then that he will soon perform an act of bravery that will be as incredible as Dhonkal's. Humming a tune to himself, he marches on.

The entire spring of 1948 had been used by the Indian Army to launch a major attack to throw the intruders right out of Kashmir. Orders came for 6 Raj. Rif., which was at Uri, to march to Tithwal to strengthen the 163 Infantry Brigade across the Nastachun Pass. The brigade was planning an offensive to dislodge the Pakistanis sitting in this sector. The pass was at 10,264 feet and the companies were deployed in areas flanked by Point 11481 on Kafir Khan Ridge that was a feature occupied by the Pakistanis.

The battalion had to move at 24 hours' notice and was to take up position on the Baniwala Dana ridge on 12 July. But a deep nala separated the ridge from where the Indian Army was positioned and the engineers had to be called in to build a bridge across this so that the soldiers could cross over. Time was at a premium and the deadline given for the bridge to be in place was the evening of 11 July.

Though all efforts were made, it was tough task and the engineers could not meet the deadline. Since the attack could not be delayed further, the engineers put a big log of wood across the nala. This was the makeshift bridge that B and D companies of 6 Raj. Rif., along with modified battalion headquarters, used to cross over on the night of 11 July.

B Company led the advance and, at 5.30 a.m. on 12 July, they managed to capture one of the features without facing any opposition from the enemy. D Company was told to pass through and secure the second feature. The attacks by 6 Raj. Rif. and 3 Royal Garhwal Rifles continued. The enemy was chased away, arms and ammunition captured and a counter-attack repulsed. Reconnaissance parties and patrols were then sent out to ascertain the enemy positions and the soldiers came back and reported that a feature called Darapari, which was at 11,481 feet, dominated the 163 Brigade-defended sector. It was heavily defended by Pakistani Army irregulars.

Just a bit further was yet another feature held by the enemy. It was felt that if the Indian Army wanted to make any further progress, Darapari and the second feature would have to be captured. The task of capturing Darapari was given to 6 Raj. Rif. under the command of Lieutenant Colonel S.S. Kallan on 16 July 1948. On 18 July, the battalion attacked along the narrow and razor-sharp ridge. This was going to be the operation where CHM Piru Singh would fight until death and secure for his battalion the coveted Darapari and also bring home the Param Vir Chakra.

18 July 1948, 1.30 a.m.

The path that leads from D Company's forward position to Darapari is barely one metre wide; on both sides are deep gorges and the soldiers are moving ahead silently in the dark; loaded rifles in their hands. D Company has been tasked with clearing Darapari and after that had been secured C Company is to move in, pass through, attack and capture the second feature. Nighttime has been chosen for the offensive deliberately so as not to alert the enemy soldiers and to take them unawares. 'Nobody will talk, light a match or even cough,' Piru Singh, whose platoon is leading the attack, tells his men and they nod in agreement. Up above somewhere are the Pakistanis, and Piru Singh is sure they have the path in their gun-sights. Alerting them to the presence of the Indian Army soldiers climbing up would be suicidal.

Though intelligence reports say that the enemy could not have had time to make proper trenches and hence it would be easy to throw them out, these reports turn out to be wrong. Unknown to the soldiers, the enemy has dug five bunkers that overlook this narrow path and had it covered completely by three medium machine guns (MMGs). The Pakistanis are also anticipating an attack and are alert, so the moment the advancing soldiers reach close to their bunkers, they open fire. D Company is trapped in this bottleneck and caught completely unaware. Bullets and shells fly in the cold night which reverberates with the screams of hit soldiers. Within a short span of 30 minutes, as many as 51 soldiers become casualty to the machine guns, grenade attacks and 2-inch and 3-inch mortars.

Suddenly there is complete chaos. If at that crucial moment,

Piru Singh does not step in and decide to put his own life at risk to further the advance of his company, the battle would be lost right then.

Piru Singh is with the forward section. Half of his men have fallen already and he can see them bleeding, limbs ripped apart, their moans filling the gaps in the din of the crossfire. Some of them are dead, others disabled by their injuries. Piru Singh himself has miraculously escaped though his clothes are singed and ripped by the grenade attacks and his arms and legs are bleeding from shrapnel injuries. He knows that the only way to tackle this attack is to silence the machine guns that are breathing fire on the mountain. Completely unmindful of his own safety, he makes a dash for the nearest bunker from where the machine-gun fire is coming. Rushing through the hail of bullets, he sprays the enemy soldiers lodged in the trench with Sten-gun fire. Before they realize he is there, he jumps in and bayonets the men handling the gun. They fall with loud screams of pain and shock and the gun falls silent.

By then the damage is done and Piru Singh realizes that all his comrades are dead. He is the only one left alive in his section. Screaming in anger, he leaps across the boulders to the next MMG post. The enemy have noticed his lone act and direct fire at him. A grenade flung at him finds its mark. It wounds him in the face and eyes but Piru Singh is beyond pain and discomfort. He doesn't notice the blood dripping down his chin and seeping into his shirt collar.

Climbing out of the trench, he wipes the blood out of his eyes and starts lobbing grenades at the next enemy position. Walking through the attacking fire, he makes his way to the second bunker and, climbing in, bayonets the two soldiers manning the second

MMG. Two of the guns have now fallen silent but he knows there is one more.

By now, he is starting to lose consciousness because of the excessive blood loss. His eyes are shutting and the blood is dripping right into them. By sheer dint of will power, Piru Singh forces his eyes to stay open. He pulls himself out of the second trench with great difficulty and shouting out the battalion war cry 'Raja Ramchandra ki Jai', he pulls out a grenade. He has not reached the third bunker when a bullet hits him in the head.

Piru Singh knows he is falling; he wants to reach the next machine gun but he no longer has any power over his limbs. Grenade in hand, he tries to walk but his legs collapse under him. Even as he drops to the ground, he manages to remove the pin from the last grenade and lobs it at the third bunker. The grenade traces an arch and as Piru Singh lies breathing his last on the ridge of Darapari, he wills his eyes to stay open. He watches the grenade find its mark. A loud blast rings out and he watches the bunker collapse, killing the enemy soldiers and silencing the MMG inside. Piru Singh Shekhawat finally closes his eyes.

C Company commander witnesses this act of heroism while directing fire in support of the attacking company. For his unmatched bravery, inspiring example and superhuman courage in the face of the enemy, CHM Piru Singh is awarded the Param Vir Chakra posthumously. The 6th Battalion, Rajputana Rifles, is awarded the Battle Honour of Darapari. In a letter to Piru Singh's mother, the then Prime Minister of India, Pandit Jawahar Lal Nehru writes: 'He paid with his life for his singularly brave act, but he left for the rest of his comrades a unique example of single-handed bravery and determined cold courage. The country is grateful for this sacrifice made in the *service of the Motherland, and it is our prayer that this may give you some peace and solace.'*

———

Piru Singh Shekhawat was born on 20 May 1918 in Rampura Beri village of Churu, Rajasthan, then Rajputana. He came from a large agricultural family and was one of seven siblings; he was the youngest of three brothers and had four sisters.

Piru began school at the age of six, but right from the beginning he did not like any kind of restriction. School became a daily punishment for this free-spirited, happy-go-lucky child and finally one day, he decided he had had enough. Flinging his slate at his teacher, Piru ran away from his classroom. He never returned, preferring to tend to the fields with his father rather than sit inside a boring, restrictive classroom. Piru was fond of hunting and roaming the forests and now had all the time for the things he loved.

The Army had always appealed to him as a career and he kept going to recruitment camps till he was selected. At 18, he joined the Army, coincidentally on his birthday—20 May 1936. He was sent to 10/1 Punjab. After training for a year at Jhelum he was posted to 5/1 Punjab. Though he had hated school, once in the Army, where he always wanted to be, Piru quickly cleared his promotional exams one after the other and soon became a lance naik and then, within a year, a naik. He was posted as an instructor in the Punjab Regimental Centre at Jhelum. In May 1945, he was appointed company havaldar major. He even went to Japan after World War II ended to serve with the Commonwealth Occupational Forces. By the time he returned in September 1947, India and Pakistan had become two countries. Being a part of the Rajput segment of 5/1 Punjab, Piru was sent to 6 Raj. Rif.

These were the terrible days when the Pakistani Army, in connivance with Pathan raiders, were attacking Jammu and Kashmir. Piru's battalion was flown to Kashmir and was part of the force used to push the raiders back beyond Uri. This was the background in which Piru Singh showed exemplary bravery and posthumously won his Param Vir Chakra.

He died on 18 July 1948. He was 30 years old.

CONGO—1961

I ndia became a founder member of the United Nations (UN) on 24 October 1945.

One of the major roles of the UN has been to bring about world peace. In this endeavour to maintain peace, the UN Peacekeeping force has unfortunately had to often resort to arms.

The Indian Army is the second largest contributor of troops to the UN missions and has taken part in as many as 31 such operations, of which Congo was one. Nearly 100 officers and men have lost their lives till now in these missions to ensure world peace. Their sacrifices often fade quickly from public memory since the soldiers die in a foreign land, fighting for a foreign country. In the UN operations in Congo, 1960, Captain Gurbachan Sigh Salaria of 3/1 Gorkha Rifles was posthumously decorated with the Param Vir Chakra.

The Congo mission of 1960 is considered one of the biggest UN missions of its time; it had under command at least 20,000 troops.

A brief background to the problem: since 1878, Congo, now Zaire, was ruled by Belgium, a country which is about one twentieth its size. In January 1960, Belgium agreed to give Congo its independence. Elections were held and in June 1960 Belgian Congo became the Democratic Republic of Congo.

There was a catch. The Congolese Army continued to be

commanded by Belgium's Lieutenant General Emile Janssens, with an all-Belgian officer force. There were no Congolese officers, which gave rise to great dissent and soon after independence, the Army declared mutiny. Congolese soldiers demanded better salaries and the expulsion of Belgian officers. There were anti-Belgian riots. The Belgians left Congo, but a civil war situation developed in the country.

Belgium quickly moved its own army into Congo, with the aim of protecting its citizens. Since this was carried out without the permission of the Congolese government, the government ordered expulsion of all Belgian troops. However, the provincial president, Moise Tshombe, announced that Katanga, the richest province of Congo, was seceding. Congo reached out for UN help and asked for military aid to protect Congo from Belgium's perceived colonial threat.

Troops of the UN Peacekeeping Mission landed in Congo in mid-July 1960 and were immediately deployed in the capital. When the UN decided that military intervention would be required to bring peace and order in Congo, India contributed a brigade of around 3000 men to the UN force.

A decision was taken to send one brigade to Congo, and 99 Infantry Brigade was picked for the task. 3/1 Gorkha Rifles was part of 99 Infantry Brigade. Most of the battalion was airlifted from Delhi to Leopoldville in Congo. The orders came suddenly and the soldiers were shifted from peacetime duties in India to a warlike situation in Congo.

After three injections, for yellow fever, cholera and tetanus, the Gorkhas left in US Air Force Globemasters that took off from Palam Airport. Major Gurbachan Salaria reached

Leopoldville on 16 March 1961. On 5 December, under orders to clear a roadblock established by the gendarmerie at a strategic roundabout at Elizabethville, Katanga, Gurbachan and two sections of brave Gorkha soldiers attacked the position frontally, and in the daring assault Captain Gurbachan Singh Salaria was killed inflicting a cutting defeat on the enemy.

The UN mission was a very complex one but it is regarded as one of the most successful even though there were many casualties on both sides. For his leadership, courage, unflinching devotion to duty and complete disregard for personal safety, Captain Gurbachan Singh Salaria was posthumously awarded the Param Vir Chakra.

Gurbachan Singh Salaria

Elizabethville, Katanga
5 December 1961, 1.12 p.m.

*Sixteen small, slim Gorkha soldiers stand quietly in the shrubbery,
their olive green combats blending in. In their hands they hold
their .303 rifles and between their teeth, their khukris, blades
glinting dangerously in the afternoon sun.*

*The soldiers are still 1500 yards from Roundabout, the location
they have been ordered to close in on. They were to approach from
the airport side, along with a troop of Swedish armoured personnel
carriers, and block the gendarmerie's withdrawal route. However,
they had run into an ambush and now have enemy fire coming
at them from a subsidiary location. Just a little way ahead stand
the hutments that have been deserted by the locals and converted
into bunkers by the revolting gendarmerie of Katanga. The enemy*

has two armoured cars and 90 men holed up in trenches and on rooftops, equipped with semi-automatic guns, far superior to the obsolete .303 rifles that the Gorkhas are using, the pre-World War II rifles painfully tedious to handle. After every round is fired, the bolt has to be pulled up and brought back to eject the cartridges and then moved forward to load fresh ones. Khukris, their traditional Nepali knives, are much, much faster. That is why the Gorkhas have unsheathed them and are now waiting for orders to attack.

'We will storm their location,' orders their company commander, Captain Gurbachan Singh Salaria, his cool, no-nonsense voice cutting through the moist heat of the afternoon.

The men get into position. They steel their hearts against all fear of death and when Salaria yells out their war cry, 'Jai Mahakali, Aayo Gorkhali', breaking into a sprint towards the enemy location, they follow.

Salaria is the first to charge. He runs across with his gun blazing, bared khukri clasped in his mouth, flashing in the sunlight. Taking on the first trench, he shoots dead the big gendarmerie on the left. From the corner of his eye he catches movement to his right, turns around and, gripping the khukri with his right hand, whips it fiercely through the air, slicing the man's horrified face. It rips off an eye and runs down his nose, slicing it into two bloody halves that bare the cartilage. Salaria's trained hand followed the standard slashing drill of right to left, left to right and, blood spraying from his lacerated face, the man falls into the trench, his intact eye still open in shock and terror.

With a snarl, Salaria turns to the next man, the blood-soaked blade glinting. He leaps into the trench and cuts the throat of the enemy soldier, who hasn't even had time to cock his rifle. A warm spray of red splashes across Salaria's sweat-soaked face. He wipes it with the sleeve of his shirt and turns to the next trench.

---

2 December 1961

Capt. Salaria, with one platoon of Alpha Company, is ordered to take over the protection duty of a refugee camp in Elizabethville. Around the same time, there is a skirmish between two drunken gendarmerie, who are trying to molest a Congolese woman, and soldiers of the peacekeeping force. It has led to a shootout. Though no one is hurt, it has resulted in the nearby gendarmerie garrison creating a roadblock and, over the following days, they manage to create a lot of trouble. Fourteen UN personnel are abducted in those days of trouble. Earlier in November, Major Ajeet, also from 3/1 Gorkha Rifles—who had been tasked to force the release of two kidnapped UN officials—had been abducted by the gendarmerie along with his driver. While Ajeet never returned, the driver's body was later found wrapped in green canvas. He had been shot at point-blank range. Ajeet had most certainly been taken hostage but all efforts to trace him were unsuccessful. He was reported missing and later declared dead.

The abduction of Ajeet is playing heavily on Salaria's mind when he goes in for the final battle. He has been seething with fury about this cowardly kidnap of a peacekeeping officer on duty. Alpha Company is guarding the refugee camp when, around 9 a.m. on 5 December, orders come for them to clear the roadblock created by the Katangese gendarmerie at Roundabout, on the route to the airport. It has to be done immediately because the block is aimed at stifling the lifeline of the UN forces that depend upon planes for not just rations, arms and ammunition, but also the evacuation of the dead and the wounded.

———

Sitting in his Dehradun house, retired Major General R.P. Singh, AVSM, VSM, who has written *A Star on the Mount of Jupiter* on Captain Salaria, giving the Indian brigade's account in the United Nations Peacekeeping Force in Congo, talks about Salaria, his voice soft. Gen R.P. was the battalion adjutant during that operation. It was the morning of 5 December 1961, he remembers, when he spoke to Salaria on the radio set and briefed him on the plan to attack and clear the Roundabout road block. In clear, concise terms he told Salaria what his orders were. He was to take a platoon of the Alpha Company and block the gendarmerie's withdrawal route, attacking them at midday, when they would be least expecting an attack.

Around 11.50 a.m. Salaria reported to him that he would be moving out of the camp in 20 minutes. The two lost contact while the platoon was moving, but, an hour later, Salaria sent a message over the radio saying he was under heavy machine-gun fire, which seemed to be coming from four different directions. He said his men were engaged in a gun battle with the enemy and that they had managed to blow up two of the enemy's armoured cars with their rocket launcher.

In his voice was a note of jubilation. This, he felt, was the moment he had been waiting for. He was very confident about what he wanted to do next. Though Maj Gen Singh remembers that he warned Salaria to assess the situation very carefully before taking any further steps, Salaria had curtly replied, 'I am going for the attack. I am sure I will win'.

'That was the last conversation he had with me,' Maj Gen Singh remembers, his gravelly voice heavy with 50-year-old memories. 'It required sheer naked courage to do what he did. Leaving his radio set and operator behind, he just charged ahead in broad daylight with his handful of Gorkhas.'

Salaria was like a man possessed. He had lost count of how many men he had killed; he'd turned into a killing machine, flinging grenades, bayoneting men and slicing through necks with his khukri. Maj Ajeet's abduction and the murder of his driver had been on his mind for many days now. He was convinced that Ajeet had been killed and his heart shrank at just how painful his death must have been. The mercenaries were cold-blooded killers with no conscience. They needed to be taught a lesson and he was going to teach as many as he could. Here and now. For him, it was a meditative moment. He lost all fear of pain or death. As he charged at the gendarmerie, all instincts of self-preservation were forgotten and he became a yogic warrior as he wreaked havoc on the battlefield.

With immense satisfaction he watched the much larger group of enemy soldiers scatter and run in terror of the tiny group of Gorkhas. They had never encountered such a ferocious enemy before. His soldiers had instilled terror with their savage charge and their deadly use of the khukri—a weapon the enemy had never seen before. In the distance, fumes were still rising from the armoured car that his men had knocked out with their rocket launcher. It was unbelievable, but they had chased away a 90-strong enemy force of men, who were bigger and equipped with the latest arms and ammunition. Around him were strewn the corpses of the gendarmerie, stunned disbelief writ large on their lifeless faces.

Salaria had just bayoneted a man who had been trying to escape, when a burst of automatic fire from another fleeing enemy soldier sprayed into his neck. He felt his neck and found it covered in blood. Two bullets had pierced his neck. The blood was seeping down and soaking his shirt. Right ahead he could see the gendarmerie running away. Some of his brave and gutsy Gorkhas were still giving chase.

He did not resist when an immense weariness enveloped him. He had lost too much blood. His task had been achieved and he was at peace. Closing his eyes, Capt. Gurbachan Singh Salaria of 3/1 Gorkha Rifles, dropped his rifle and fell, drifting into unconsciousness from which he would never awaken.

Many years earlier, when Salaria had joined the Gorkha Rifles, he had been told that his regiment's motto was: It is better to die than to be a coward: 'Kafar hunu bhanda marnu ramro.'

Salaria had lived up to the motto.

Salaria fancied himself a palmist. Before the Congo deployment in February 1961, he had visited Chotta Shimla for some work and run into an excise officer, who used to read people's palms.

Reading Salaria's hand, the officer told him that there was a star on his mount of Jupiter, which would bring him great fame. Salaria took the prediction very seriously and would often point it out to fellow officers in lighter moments. Maj Gen R.P. Singh remembers how in Congo one day when he and Salaria were discussing the abduction of Maj Ajeet by enemy soldiers, and hoping that Ajeet would be returned to them unharmed, Salaria told him quite seriously that he had read Ajeet's hand and that he had a clear break in his lifeline. He quickly added though that Ajeet also had a supporting lifeline so nothing should happen to him.

He then went on to show the general his own right hand. He again pointed out the star on his mount of Jupiter. 'Wait and see, this star will take me to great heights,' he said. Singh had leaned over to feel the mount, but only out of politeness. 'I just shrugged it off as I never took his knowledge of palmistry seriously,' the general recounts. 'I did not know that his day of reckoning and attaining fame was just a few days away. Or that he would never know of this fame since it would come when he was in his heavenly abode,' he says quietly.

Instead he just told Salaria that no one could stop anyone from achieving fame if it was written in their destiny. Soon after Salaria left after refusing a dinner offer, Singh took out a copy of Cheiro's book on palmistry that he had in his suitcase and read about the star on the mount of Jupiter. 'These people are ambitious, fearless and determined in all that they undertake. They are leaders. They concentrate on whatever they may be doing at that moment and see no way but their own,' said the book. A cold shiver ran down Singh's spine. He knew just how upset and angry Salaria was about Ajeet's abduction and just how keen he was to teach the gendarmerie a lesson. A concerned Singh went down to the control room and asked the operator to check if Salaria had reached his location safely. He heaved a sigh of relief when confirmation came that he had.

———

Gurbachan Singh Salaria was born on 29 November 1935 in a village called Janwal, near Shakargarh, now in Pakistan. The second of five children, he was a favourite of his grandmother, who would tie a black thread around his waist to keep the evil eye away from him. By that time, Adolf Hitler had already emerged as a dark force and war clouds were looming over the world.

Gurbachan's father Munshi Ram was in the Armoured Corps of the British Indian Army and would move from one Army cantonment to another, coming home only on annual or casual leave. When he did come home it was celebration time in the family. His favourite food would be cooked, the house would sparkle and friends and family drop in to listen to his awe-inspiring tales of faraway places where soldiers performed great acts of bravery. Little Gurbachan and his siblings would listen to their father in rapt attention as he sat smoking his hookah. Quite possibly this is how Gurbachan was inspired to be courageous.

Gurbachan's mother Dhan Devi had never been to school and was completely occupied with her growing children. She was, however, very particular that her children's education did not suffer despite living in a village. Gurbachan would go to school regularly, but was always more occupied with games and outdoor activities rather than studying. He was a good kabaddi player, and continued to be good at sports even after he cleared the entrance to King George's Royal Military College (KGRMC), Bangalore, at 11 years of age. Though he was initially rejected in the physical exam because his chest was found to be an inch less than the stipulated measurements, he was given a month to try again. He took the challenge head on, drinking one litre of goat's milk every day and exercising passionately.

When he went back for his medical, he had managed to increase his chest by two-and-a-half inches and was immediately admitted. He joined the college in August 1946 as a cadet. In 1947, he was transferred to KGRMC Jullundur, which was closer to his village.

When he was in his second year, Gurbachan and a friend were once bullied and insulted by another cadet. Gurbachan's self-respect took a blow but he challenged the bully to a boxing match the next day. He boxed with such fury that the bully was knocked out and had to apologize. The operation in Congo was very reminiscent of this incident; where Gurbachan took on a much bigger and better equipped enemy fighting force just because he wanted to teach them a lesson in war ethics.

Gurbachan went on to the National Defence Academy and then the Indian Military Academy. He joined 2/3 Gorkha Rifles in July 1954 where because of his cropped hair cut and upturned moustache he was nicknamed Khan Saheb by his commanding officer. In March 1960, he received orders transferring him to 3/1 Gorkha Rifles. And that was where General R.P. Singh, who was then the battalion adjutant, met him.

General Singh found Salaria to be a simple man, spartan and very careful with money, unlike other young officers, many of whom had extravagant tastes. In fact, Salaria once told him, he recalled, that he was sending money home to finance the education of his younger brother Sukhdev, at college in Jammu.

Sukhdev is now 75 and lives in Pathankot. He is bedridden and has lost his sense of balance, but he remembers fondly how, when he and Gurbachan were little boys—Gurbachan was older by two years—they would go swimming in the small stream that ran across their village. 'We had no worries then; we would splash around in the stream. What beautiful days they were. Now Gurbachan is gone and I can't walk, but whenever I think of him that is the first memory that streams into my head,' says the old man, sinking back into silence. He has more memories to recount but his strength fails him.

This story is based on conversations with Major General (Retd) R.P. Singh, AVSM, VSM, who has written *A Star on the Mount of Jupiter*, a book on Captain Salaria, giving the Indian brigade's account in the United Nations Peacekeeping Force in Congo.

THE INDO–CHINESE
WAR OF 1962

The blunder committed by political as well as military leadership by misreading the Chinese game and neglecting the Indian Army's preparedness, made India suffer a humiliating defeat in the Sino-Indian war. The only thing that stood out was the iron will and cold courage of the soldiers who, though completely outnumbered and ill-equipped, fought to defend their country's honour.

The seeds of the war were sown in the Aksai Chin area which India considered a part of Kashmir but China considered a part of Xinjiang. Tension was compounded further after the Tibetan uprising of 1959, when India granted asylum to the Dalai Lama. This led to unpleasantness with China and some violent incidents on the border.

India then started sending patrols into disputed areas with China. The aim was to create outposts behind the advancing Chinese Army so that their supplies could be cut off. India initiated a Forward Policy in which it placed outposts along the border. These included some posts which were placed north of the McMohan Line, the eastern part of the Line of Actual Control.

Initially, the plan seemed to work but later China took this as a threat and decided to teach India a lesson. A romantic and politically shortsighted Nehru however did not increase military spending on preparation for a possible war with China. Not only was the Army denied equipment, the renowned 4th Infantry Division was used to build houses instead of preparing for war.

Nehru appointed Lt General B.M. Kaul as Chief of Army Staff in 1961. General Kaul was confident that China would not retaliate when India sent patrols into areas disputed with China. The Chinese, however, slowly started encircling the Indian positions.

Maj Dhan Singh Thapa's post at Sirijap in Ladakh was one such case. In fact, such was the confidence that China would not attack that he had even been granted leave to go home just a few days before the Chinese attacked Sirijap.

Major Thapa was waiting for his reliever when the Chinese attacked, massacring nearly the entire company and taking the survivors back as Prisoners of War. Maj Thapa, awarded a Param Vir Chakra posthumously since he was believed dead, was one of these POWs.

As early as August, China had started accumulating arms, ammunition and rations and the signs were clear that they were preparing for war. India, however, turned a blind eye to all this. Subedar Joginder Singh, awarded a Param Vir Chakra posthumously, waited across a stream in the Bumla axis in Arunachal Pradesh, then called the North-East Frontier Agency, watching the Chinese prepare their defences.

Indian forces were unprepared, ill-equipped and did not even have proper winter clothing when on 12 October Jawaharlal Nehru declared that he had ordered the Indian Army to throw the Chinese out of NEFA. On 14 October, an editorial in the *People's Daily* in China issued a warning to India and Nehru, 'At this critical moment, we still want to appeal once more to Mr Nehru: better rein in at the edge of the precipice and do not use the lives of Indian troops as stakes in your gamble,' it said. On 20 October, the Chinese People's Liberation Army launched two attacks on India. One of these was in Thag La, NEFA, while the other was in the Chushul sector of Ladakh. Both the attacks were massive in terms of troop concentration. On the Indian side, single companies of around 120 soldiers defended posts that were surrounded by thousands of enemy soldiers armed with machine guns, mortars and grenades. The Battle of Rezang La, where almost every man died fighting and Major Shaitan Singh got his Param Vir Chakra posthumously, is still remembered as a tale of tragic heroism where brave soldiers unquestioningly gave up their lives for the mistakes of shaky government heads and bad military leaders.

The Sino-Indian War was fought at altitudes over 14,000 feet. The lessons learnt from it were: good intelligence and war readiness are imperative to winning wars, good command at the senior level means generals be appointed on military merit and not sycophancy, politicians should not ignore the advice of military officers regarding military readiness, and that incompetent people who rise to the top mess up nations.

The only shining stars of the '62 war were the brave soldiers of the Indian Army, who fought valiantly and often to death to protect their territories. The Indian soldiers lacked everything except courage, it has been famously said. These brave hearts fought in high attitudes and freezing temperatures. They used old and cumbersome .303 rifles against Chinese automatics. They were outnumbered and completely mauled by the well-prepared Chinese Army but they continued to fight for the honour of their nation.

Many brave stories of unassuming heroes in uniform came out of this war. Three of them were of Subedar Joginder Singh, Maj Dhan Singh Thapa and Maj Shaitan Singh. All three were awarded the Param Vir Chakra posthumously but miraculously Maj Thapa returned from the dead a few months after the Battle of Sirijap. He had been taken Prisoner of War by the Chinese.

Their brave tales of unbelievable courage and fortitude tell us how soldiers don't forget their responsibilities even if politicians do.

Dhan Singh Thapa

Battle For Sirijap 1, Ladakh Region
20 October 1962

*The Gorkha soldier is in his early 20s. He is firing from his
trench. His slim fingers hold the .303 rifle so close to his slight
frame that it appears to be an extension of his body. A helmet
covers his young face.*

*It is freezing cold but there are beads of sweat on his brow. He
is shooting at the Chinese, who are coming in a massive wave,
their automatic rifles spraying bullets blindly at the men defending
Sirijap 1. The post lies on the northern edge of the Pangong Tso
and is manned by the Delta Company of the first battalion of 8
Gorkha Rifles.*

*The soldier uses his bullets with care. He knows ammunition
is running short and he and his comrades are completely*

outnumbered. There were 28 of them when the Chinese started shelling at 6 a.m. but nearly half of them now lie around him, some dead, others dying.

Just then, a shell blows up a bunker that collapses right on top of Subedar Min Bahadur Gurung, the company second-in-command. Gurung Sahab crawls out of the debris, injured and bleeding, light machine gun (LMG) still in his hand. He starts firing at the enemy again, his mud-streaked face a mask of cold control. Major Dhan Singh Thapa, commander, D Company, continues to move from trench to trench, inspiring those left of his men to be brave.

Just then a bullet hits the soldier in the hand. He drops the rifle and, screaming with pain, runs into the tent that still stands intact. Without losing a second, Maj Thapa reaches for the fallen gun and carries it inside. He finds the terrified soldier cringing in a corner, nursing his injured hand.

Thapa walks across to him and pats him on the head softly. 'Kafar hunu bhanda marnu ramro' (It is better to die than be a coward), he says, handing the gun back to the young man. 'If we have to die we'll all die together, but kill a few before you die.'

With that Maj Thapa turns around and quickly makes his way back to where a soldier lies dead with his LMG still in his hands. He pulls the gun and gets into the trench himself, positioning himself in front of the advancing enemy. From the corner of his eye he sees the injured soldier walking back with a determined look on his face and the rifle in his blood-stained hands.

The battle that took place at Sirijap 1 in the Chushul sector of Ladakh is immortalized in military history for the dynamic leadership of Maj Dhan Singh Thapa. He was the man who inspired his brave Gorkhas to fight to the last.

Sirijap 1 was one of the many posts established as part of the forward policy that had been employed by India to counter the Chinese, who had been establishing posts in Ladakh. Since the men of D Company had to be split among a number of posts, only about 28 soldiers were placed at Sirijap 1. A Chinese attack wasn't really expected there and the Major, who had gone to Ladakh leaving his pregnant wife behind in Dehradun, had even been granted one week's leave to go home and the officer sent to relieve him had reached Leh. But despite getting permission to proceed on leave, Thapa had insisted upon waiting for his replacement to take over Sirijap since he did not want to leave his company headless.

On 19 October, Maj Thapa was surprised to find hectic activity on the enemy side and build-up of the Chinese forces on the posts. Suspecting a possible attack, Maj Thapa and his men began preparing their defence. The ground was hard and frozen and it was very difficult to dig in so they piled up sandbags to reinforce their bunkers.

The men waited anxiously that entire night. There were just 28 of them! But Maj Thapa inspired them with his words of courage. 'Don't forget that one Gorkha is equal to 10 others,' he told them with quiet confidence.

'We did not panic in any way, neither were we afraid of anything except the biting cold outside the trenches, where freezing winds would blow during our patrols at night,' Subedar Major Tulsi Ram Thapa, a survivor, will tell Poonam (Maj Thapa's youngest daughter) many years later when she is researching for a biography on her father). 'We had enough clothing. Each of us was issued three pairs of woollen socks, woollen undergarments, trousers, goggles, jackets, sleeping bags, camouflage raincoats, etc., and physically we were quite comfortable. Some of us had even received letters from home.'

That dark night passed without any untoward incident and slowly the soldiers who were not on duty closed their eyes for some rest. At 6 a.m. on 20 October, there was a blast and Sirijap 1 shook under heavy artillery fire. Bombs exploded and the air rang with the deadly hiss of shells and screams of those hit, followed by the boom of heavy mortars. The explosions destroyed the bunkers the Gorkhas had constructed and caused devastation amongst their small force. Many soldiers were killed in their trenches, many more wounded. Very soon the radio network was also disrupted, cutting the company off completely from the rest of the battalion.

Signal officer Maj Ved Vyas will later remember the last message received from Maj Thapa. 'Neither will I withdraw, nor will I surrender,' he had said.

The observation post at Tokung, a ferry point for boats that were used for the maintenance of posts in the Pangong Tso area, was the only place from where soldiers could witness the battle of Sirijap. The soldiers say the shelling went on for more than two hours and Sirijap looked like it had been set on fire.

While the shelling was on, the Chinese Army managed to get close to the company position. No sooner had the shelling stopped than they attacked in a strength of more than 500. The Gorkhas put up a very brave fight. Most of them were in their early 20s with just a few years of service. Their LMGs and .303s were no match for the sophisticated arms and ammunition with the enemy, but they still managed to create havoc in the Chinese army. Small and slim in stature, they did not lack in courage. Led by their company commander, who was himself just 33 years old, they fixed the enemy soldiers in their gun-sights and shot them down the moment they came close.

The sheer numbers of the Chinese, however, were overwhelming. Every time they repulsed an advance the enemy would attack in even larger numbers. Naik Krishna Bahadur Thapa, in charge of one section, was hit by a splinter that severed his leg. In spite of his grievous wound, he picked up the LMG of a dead comrade and continued to fire at the advancing enemy till he was hit by another volley of bullets and dropped dead.

The men who survived remember how Maj Thapa rose above all others. He proved to them that he was a true commander. While the firing was on, he boldly went around bunkers without a thought for his own safety, strengthening breaches, replacing men who had died or were injured and encouraging the remaining with his brave words. He inspired them to hang on courageously and not bother about what was bound to happen.

After two of their attacks were repelled, the Chinese used amphibious crafts to ferry machine guns and bazookas across the lake. Since D Company had lost all radio contact, the battalion headquarters sent Naik Rabilal Thapa with two boats on the lake to find out what was happening, but the Chinese fired at them and managed to capsize one, drowning all men on board. The other returned to the battalion with Naik

Rabilal on board. He had managed to get within 1000 yards of Sirijap before the enemy opened LMG fire at him from three sides. He saw clouds of grey smoke and flames rising from Sirijap which appeared totally destroyed. He reported that the post had fallen to the Chinese and all men defending it had lost their lives.

The fact was that Sirijap had not lost all its men. Seven of the brave soldiers were still holding on though they were fast running out of ammunition. Inspired by the example of their company commander, who continued to fight by their side, they did not lose their nerve. Those who ran out of bullets picked up the rifles of their dead comrades and kept firing.

When all their ammunition finished and the Chinese started using incendiary bombs to start fires to smoke out the soldiers, the Gorkhas pulled out their khukris (traditional Nepali knives), and jumped out of their trenches screaming out their war cry: 'Jai Mahakali, Aayo Gorkhali.' Led by their commander, they plunged their deadly blades deep into enemy throats and chests. Maj Thapa was one of the last few left alive and was fighting with his khukri when he was hit in the face by a rifle butt and lost two of his teeth. He killed the Chinese soldier and was in the process of putting out a fire by rolling over it physically when he was surrounded and taken prisoner along with a few others.

When dusk fell over Sirijap on 20 October, the battalion had no idea about the fate of Maj Thapa, who had been given up as dead along with the 28 other heroes. For his devotion to duty, undaunted gallantry and inspiring command, Maj Thapa was recommended for an immediate award of Param

Vir Chakra (PVC). He was awarded the PVC posthumously since he was believed to have been killed in the war.

───────

Unknown to his battalion, the Major and a few other survivors of Sirijap were taken away by the Chinese, first to Khurnak Fort and subsequently to Sinkiang, as prisoners of war (POWs). Maj Thapa remained in Chinese captivity till May 1963. He was kept in complete isolation, subjected to Chinese propaganda, which included being made to watch Chinese films that glorified their policies, and being weakened emotionally by being told that despite knowing that they were alive, the Indian Army and the government were not taking any interest in their release.

He might have spent his entire life in custody had he not made friends with a Chinese boy who brought him meals in the tent where he was prisoner. Even though he could not speak Chinese Maj Thapa established a bond with this boy and managed to convey to him that he had a family in India, his wife was pregnant and he wanted to send them a letter telling them he was alive. The Chinese boy posted the letter for him and it reached Major Thapa's maternal uncle in Simla, who brought it to the notice of the Army that the PVC awardee, who had been declared dead, was in fact alive and in Chinese captivity.

When Maj Thapa was brought back, he recounted tales of how he was continuously pressurized to admit that he was surrendering to the Chinese and when he did not succumb, he was made to walk from one post to another in the freezing cold, without shoes and with a radio set strapped onto his back. He suffered from frostbite because of this continuous exposure to snow. Poornima says that her father suffered all his life from swollen feet and joint pain that later developed into arthritis.

Maj Thapa did not like to talk about his days as a prisoner and hardly ever spoke about the war either. 'When we badgered him he would just say that he could never forget the sight of his soldiers dying in front of his eyes one by one or overcome the humiliation of being a POW,' Poornima says.

After Dhan Singh had been reported dead, his family had performed all his death rituals though his wife Shukla kept insisting that her husband was alive and would come back; he had promised her he would take her with him to his next posting. When Gorkha officers came to her house on 12 Young Road in Dehradun after the war with black bands on their uniforms to break the news of her husband's death, she refused to believe them. At that time everyone felt she was under shock. When Maj Thapa came back in May 1963, he had to be remarried to Shukla since she had been made to undergo the rituals of widowhood. He also found himself face to face with his newborn son Param Deep Thapa, who had been named after the PVC his father had been awarded. When he grew up, Param went on to join the Army.

Maj Thapa rose to the rank of Lieutenant Colonel and served till he retired. He continued to attend almost all the Republic Day parades from 1964 to 2004. Sick and undergoing dialysis for kidney failure in Delhi, Lt Col Thapa would slip in and out of consciousness in his last year. Poornima, who was taking care of him, pleaded with him to not attend the parade that year, but he refused gently yet firmly. 'When I wear my uniform and go for the parade, I represent my soldiers; those men who fought a war with me. I cannot let them down,' he told her. Though he could hardly stand for long or even stay alert, he put on his uniform, pinned on his PVC, tilted his Gorkha hat at the perfect angle and went for the parade, remembers Poornima. Through sheer willpower, he managed to stand in the jeep till he had saluted the President. After that, he sat down.

That would be the last Republic Day parade he would attend. On 5 September 2005, Lt Col Thapa died of kidney failure. He was 77 years old.

———

Dhan Singh Thapa was born on 28 April 1928 in Simla, Himachal Pradesh, and commissioned into 8 Gorkha Rifles on 28 August 1949. Gentle and unassuming by temperament, he was, however, passionate about football, a sport he could not play later in life when he began to suffer from arthritis.

He was a brave man. Even before the '62 war, when he was battling insurgency in Nagaland, his wife remembers how he would go out on night patrols without a thought for his own safety. In fact, Shukla delivered their second daughter at home at night when he was out on an operation in insurgency-hit Mochungchung, Nagaland. They lost their daughter just a few months before he went for the war; Thapa left behind his pregnant and grieving wife. Though duty came first, he was an indulgent father and a devoted husband, happy to hear his wife sing in parties and at home.

Simple and straightforward, he followed his heart. He loved the men who worked under him more than he loved those above him. Deeply religious, he enjoyed reading books on philosophy. When he was in captivity, the Chinese asked him why he believed in God. He said, 'I should have been killed in the war, but it is a miracle that I'm still alive.' He then opened his jacket and told the interrogating officer, 'You can try to shoot me if you want but if God doesn't want me to die, I won't.'

The Chinese did not shoot him and, the fact is that he did return from the dead for his people.

This story has been reconstructed from accounts of retired soldiers and conversations with Poonam Thapa, late Lt Col Dhan Singh Thapa, PVC's daughter.

Joginder Singh

About 45 km from Bathinda, across the lush green fields that are ripe with wheat, is a small village called Chehalanwalan. There in a large brick house is an eclectic mix of people and things: a shiny tractor, a lovingly polished Gypsy, an old cell phone with a loud Bollywood ringtone, a couple of noisily bleating goats, sour lassi, and an old bent Biji (grandmother) with a toothless smile.

This is a joint family of many and at their head is 81-year-old Subedar Kala Singh, who retired from the Army more than 30 years ago. The proud sardar, who stands tall in his white pathan suit, doesn't wear the olive green uniform anymore. Yet, no one would doubt that he is a soldier. He is one of the three men who came back alive from the battle of Tongpen La, near Bum La, Tawang, in the North-East Frontier Agency (NEFA) in 1962.

Kala Singh is one of the last persons to have seen Param Vir Chakra Joginder Singh alive. He is the only person who can tell us about this bravest of the brave who charged at a brigade strength of Chinese with just 29 men by his side. He can also tell us of the man who not only inspired his soldiers to bravery, but also led them to a glorious death after ammunition ran out and they fought with bayonets fixed to their guns.

Joginder Singh was the bravest of the brave and he lived exactly the way he asked his men to: like a lion, 'sher ke maafik'.

But to understand that we must start from where old man Kala's story begins: on a very cold day on a ridge in Bum La, where a platoon of 1 Sikh commanded by Subedar Joginder Singh watched warily as a thousand-plus Chinese soldiers dug trenches and lined up just 250 yards away, across a shallow stream that gurgled between the two armies. A bloody battle was waiting to be fought.

October 1962

Kala was 27 and in Lucknow to participate in a basketball tournament when it became imminent that there was going to be war with China. All the matches were cancelled and he was told to join his battalion, which had just been moved to NEFA—now the state of Arunachal Pradesh. Kala says that he took the train to Missamari in Assam and then hitched a ride to Tawang on 11 October. Two days later he was told to join his company and, on 14 October, sent to join Sub Joginder Singh's platoon on the Bum La axis.

More than a fortnight passed after 1 Sikh had reached there. They had been moved straight from Jaipur when war seemed unavoidable. When the orders came, the soldiers had packed their boxes, taken the train to Missamari, and got on to Army trucks heading for Tawang. They had made a long and tiring journey through the forests of Arunachal, with its orchids drooping down from lush green trees; they crossed the claustrophobic Tenga valley, climbed the winding path to Bomdila and then descended to beautiful Dhirang, where women worked with runny-nosed pink-cheeked babies strapped to their backs. Driving across the mist-blurred Sela Pass at 13,714 feet, they crossed the frozen Sela Lake. Finally they had got onto a narrow track cut into fallen snow to reach Tawang.

They were going there to fight a war.

Most of the battalion had never seen the area before, and walked to their designated posts and companies. Many of the soldiers and officers were still on leave or on posting. Since the orders for the move had come suddenly, many of the platoons were short of their normal strength. They also did not have adequate winter clothing or modern equipment to fight. It was a war fought on courage alone. 'Sipahiyon ka dil tha jo woh ladne gaye,' (Only a soldier's heart could spur them to fight) says Kala, his voice thick with emotion. He himself did not have a jacket or proper winter boots or gloves.

Since Sub Joginder Singh's experience in World War II and the war with Pakistan in 1947–48 made him a highly respected man in the battalion, he was handpicked to be sent forward. Soon after reaching the assigned spot, he and his platoon of 29 men had dug trenches on the ridge and settled down to await further orders.

As war clouds loomed, they saw Assam Rifles soldiers trudging back—a standard drill. Assam Rifles and paramilitary forces would move back and make way for the Army when wars were fought.

'We would see them marching to safer zones while we were setting up camp and digging trenches. They would tell us, "ladai hone wali hai, ab hamara kaam khatam, aap ka kaam shuru (the war is about to begin, our job is done; you have work ahead of you),"' remembers Kala.

On 20 October, the Chinese attacked the Indian post at Namka Chu that was under 7th Infantry Brigade. Equipped with the latest arms and ammunition and having readied for war for close to three years, they brutally massacred the Indian troops. The single-shot World War II vintage rifles that the Indian soldiers were using were no match for the automatic rifles with the Chinese soldiers. The Indian soldiers did not have proper winter clothing either while the Chinese were fully prepare for battle.After their first victory, the Chinese crossed into Indian territory and marched all the way to where Joginder Singh and his men had established their post. They began to collect at the other bank of the stream and to dig trenches. The stream was about two-and-a-half foot deep and, if they wanted, the soldiers could walk across quite easily. As the Chinese built up their numbers and strengthened their bunkers, Joginder Singh and his men began to feel uneasy. According to Kala, when he called up for orders for him and his platoon, he was told, 'You will stay there till the last bullet and fight. Aap aakhri goli tak ladenge.'

The men had accepted this with courage and prepared themselves mentally for war. Every morning they would wake up to spot some new activity on the Chinese side; they would spend the day sharing memories of home and loved ones and night in fitful sleep, expecting an attack any minute.

Kala was in the trench that functioned as the langar (cookhouse). It was at a height on the ridge and at some distance from where the rest of the platoon was stationed. Next to it in a wooden shack were the rations and stores; Kala had gone there to take an inventory so that things that were falling short could be ordered on the radio set. The soldiers had been getting meat and fresh vegetables like cauliflower and potatoes regularly, they still got plenty of lentils, but the milk had stopped coming ever since tension had built up. The men were drinking tea with spoonfuls of milk stirred in. The condensed milk would come in one-pound tins from the Verka dairy back home in Punjab, remembers Kala. 'Sometimes we would mix hot water in it and drink it as milk. I still remember the tin with its picture of a lady on it; it was so sweet that we never had to add sugar.'

Often Joginder Singh would come up to the cookhouse in the afternoon and talk to Kala about the possibility that he could die in that war just a year before his retirement. 'But we cannot run away from this, Kale. What face will we show our families? Kahenge gaddaar aa gaye. We'll be dubbed traitors for the rest of our lives,' he would say and Kala would agree. The two would then lose themselves in memories of the time

they had spent together in the paltan (battalion). The evening
before the final battle of his life Joginder Singh had sent his
sahayak to fetch his bottle of rum from the stores. 'Sahab has
asked me to get him his bottle of rum. He said: "Kal din chade,
na chade, hum zinda bachen ya na bachen, ek botal rum padi
hai, pee lein usse (We may or may not survive to see the next
morning, one bottle of rum remains, let me finish it)."'

Kala had handed over the bottle. 'Maine bhej di thi. Shayad
pee li hogi (I sent it. He must have drunk it),' he says.

The next morning the Chinese attacked.

---

23 October 1962, 5.30 a.m.

*The first wave of Chinese attack comes just a few minutes after the
langari or cook Bahadur Singh leaves the cookhouse with thermos
flasks holding freshly brewed steaming hot tea for the platoon.*

*Sub Kala Singh does not hear the gunfire since the soldiers'
trenches are much lower on the ridge. But the rest of the men
reach for their guns as a large force of the Chinese start to cross
the stream, their rugged boots splashing across the water. They
come in waves of hundreds.*

*Led by their fearless commander, the brave men of 1 Sikh stand
their ground and face the first attack bravely. From their trenches
they take on the enemy soldiers, fixing them within the sight of
their rifles and shooting them through their heads and hearts.*

*The first attack is successfully repulsed. The enemy is temporarily
halted because of the high casualty. However, within half-an-hour
they unleash a second attack with more troops. War cries ring out*

and Joginder Singh inspires his men with his words and action. Roaring like a lion, he keeps up the defence and implores his men to be quick and precise with their bullets. He is wounded in the thigh, and continuing to inspire his men, refuses to be evacuated. Despite being completely outnumbered, the troops stubbornly hold on to their position and do not withdraw an inch.

In the meanwhile, communication with the company post is also lost.

Ammunition is falling short; the old, single-shot loading rifles with the Sikhs are no match for the sophisticated weapons of the Chinese, but they still cannot overrun the post.

So, they launch a third wave of attack. By now, nearly half the men in the platoon have been killed and ammunition is very short. Despite his injury, Joginder Singh himself mans a light machine gun and shoots down as many of the enemy soldiers as he can. Soon, the men run completely out of ammunition.

The Chinese are still coming at them. When death becomes imminent, Joginder Singh tells the men it is time to prove themselves. They fix bayonets on their guns, jump out of their trenches and rush into the charging enemy soldiers with loud cries of 'Bole so nihal, sat sri Akal'.

The Chinese are stunned by the courage of these hugely outnumbered, but spirited, Sikh warriors with their flowing beards and their turbans. They have never beheld such a sight before.

Led by the slim and quick Joginder Singh, the surviving men charge head-on into the Chinese columns. The air rings out with screams and cries of the soldiers hurling abuse at each other. As the Chinese keep coming at them with guns blazing, none of the Sikhs tries to run or hide. Drawing courage from

Joginder Singh, they rush in and bayonet as many as they can before they finally fall under enemy fire. Eventually, every single man collapses.

As the sun sets that evening, Joginder Singh, the brave Sikh soldier, disabled by his injuries, lies on the Bum La axis, the softly falling snow covering his body gently. But Joginder Singh does not die then. He is carried away by the Chinese, who return with mules the next day. He dies in captivity. His body is never returned.

When the Chinese hear over the radio that the Indian government is awarding a PVC to Sub Joginder Singh, they reverently return his ashes. Sub Kala Singh carries these to Sub Joginder Singh's village and hands them over to his wife. The brave JCO's daughter had died of shock the day she heard of her father's sacrifice, he discovers.

If Joginder Singh had not been killed in the war, he would have hung up his uniform in a year's time and gone back to his wife and children in his sunny village near Moga in Punjab, with a monthly pension of Rs 116. Perhaps he would have still been farming wheat there while recounting war stories to his grandchildren about the day the Chinese attacked his platoon on an ice-cold ridge near Bum La.

———

Kala has many memories of Joginder Saab. He was a proud man, he remembers. He would normally speak Punjabi but break into Urdu whenever he got angry. He would not hesitate to pull up the men under his command or even take a stand with senior officers. 'Kadak jyada tha Saab (Sir was very stern),' chuckles Kala, recounting an incident that took place in 1959, when 1 Sikh was at Jaipur.

There was much excitement in the air, he says, because Queen Elizabeth was to visit. Sub Joginder Singh was the parade-in-charge and had been holding very strict practice for the 90 men under his command. After one such rigorous practice, he announced a rest of 10 minutes. The men broke the lines and dispersed happily but, much to Joginder Singh's annoyance, were late in coming back. 'You had been given a rest and should have come back running,' he told the men and then pointed to a tree in the distance. 'Sab uske bayen se jaayenge and daayen se aayenge (All will go from its left and return from the right),' he shouted, sending the men on a punishment run.

While going around the tree, one of the soldiers ran past a drum left behind by the band and couldn't resist hitting it. When Joginder Saab heard the drum he was livid and asked for the culprit to own up. No one did. This made him even angrier and he told the men to put their weapons on the ground and start crawling on their stomach and elbows. Gursharan Singh, a footballer, was seen as the chief suspect but he refused to confess saying he was too scared of the punishment Joginder Saab would give him if he was found out!

In another incident around the same time, an officer inspecting the cookhouse found some jawans on duty with nails longer than the prescribed length. Joginder Saab was summoned and pulled up. He tried explaining to the officer that since he was also in charge of the parade, he had been unable to find time for both the tasks. This just angered the officer further and picking up a fistful of sand, he blew on it saying: 'Tujhe rait ki tarah uda doonga (I will blow you up like sand)'.

Joginder Singh looked the officer in the eye, pointed a finger to the sky and then placed the tip at his forehead saying: 'Jab tak woh nahi chaahe aap mera kuch nahi bigaad sakte (You cannot harm me as long as He does not desire it)'.

The officer left in a huff, but soon realized he had been disrespectful to a proud, battle-hardy soldier. He called Joginder Singh to his office the next day; the two hugged each other and promised to forget the squabble.

Joginder Singh was born on 28 September 1921 in Mahakalan village near Moga in Punjab. His parents were not well off and could not afford a good education for him. As a result he could not finish school and decided to join the Army.

He was recruited into 1 Sikh and fulfilled his desire for education by clearing professional exams and becoming a unit instructor. He was a very strict disciplinarian and instilled respect in the troops under his command. When he was in his early 30s, he got married and had a son and two daughters.

Joginder Singh died fighting a shamefully unequal battle his government pushed him into, completely unprepared and unequipped, but he is immortalized in the country's history for his brave act of valour.

This story was reconstructed from the memories of Sub (Retd) Kala Singh

Shaitan Singh

It is February 1963. A few months after the war with China is over, a Ladakhi shepherd grazing his herd in no-man's land finds his way to Rezang La in Chushul, quite by chance. The destroyed bunkers, empty shells and used gun-cartridges scattered around tell him that he has stumbled upon the location of conflict. And then he notices the bodies. These are of dead soldiers in uniform, some still holding their weapons, faces twisted in pain. The extreme cold has preserved them in the moment that death claimed them. Their vacant eyes stare across space and time, a mute witness to their dying moments. These dead men speak of the terrible carnage that befell them. Speechless with horror, the shepherd runs down and informs the closest Indian Army picket.

Accompanied by Press Information Bureau officials, 13 Kumaon sends out a group of men, who recognize their comrades. The bodies are of the soldiers of the Charlie Company, 13 Kumaon, commanded by Major Shaitan Singh, which was almost completely wiped out by the Chinese in the Battle of Rezang La on 18 November 1962. Every single soldier they find is dead from multiple bullet wounds, shell injuries or splinters. Some lie dead in their bunkers, buried under boulders, others are still holding on to the butts of blown-off rifles. The nursing assistant has a syringe in his hand and a roll of bandage, the soldier operating the mortar holds a bomb.

Maj Shaitan Singh is lying by a rock, a blood-stained bandage on his left arm, his stomach ripped open by a machine gun burst. The battle-hardy Brigadier T.N. Raina, commander, 114 Infantry Brigade, is so overcome by emotion that he breaks down. The orders for every man to fight till the last round and the last bullet had come from him.

What is most remarkable is that none of the men has a bullet in his back. This means no one tried to run away. While Maj Shaitan Singh's body is sent back to Jodhpur, the other heroes of Rezang La are cremated with full military honours at High Ground, the place where the battalion headquarters (HQ) used to be at the time of the battle. Mass funeral pyres are lit. 13 Kumaon is later awarded the Battle Honour Rezang La and the Theatre Honour Ladakh 1962. These names continue to remind new generations of soldiers of the story of Maj Shaitan Singh and his brave men who died defending their country's honour. C Company is later re-raised and designated Rezang La Company by Army Headquarters.

Of the 124 men deployed at Rezang La, 113 died fighting. Five were taken prisoners of war, of whom one died in custody. Only six survivors found their way back to their battalion of whom two live in Rewari, Haryana, about 80 km from Delhi.

Subedar (Honorary Captain) Ram Chander and Havaldar Nihal Singh, Sena Medal, both 74 and wearing the green-and-yellow-striped regimental cravats of the Kumaonis, meet me at the Rezang La memorial in Rewari. Since 13 Kumaon was an all-Ahir paltan, most men who died in Rezang La belonged to villages in that area, and the memorial, which holds earth brought from where they fought their last battle, is dedicated to them.

Ram Chander was Maj Shaitan Singh's radio operator, and one of the last people to see him alive. Nihal was on the light machine gun (LMG); he rolls up his shirtsleeves to show me the terrible scars of enemy bullets that pierced his arms when he was swinging his gun left to right. He was the only one left alive in his trench.

It is from these men that I hear the amazing story of Maj Shaitan Singh and the Vir Ahirs of C Company, 13 Kumaon.

Rezang La
October 1962

When a Chinese attack became imminent in Ladakh, 13 Kumaon was one of the battalions to be moved there under 114 Infantry Brigade, which had been tasked with defending Chushul. They reached Leh on 2 October and were moved to Chushul after about ten days. C Company was told to establish posts at a pass called Rezang La, about 30 km south of the village of Chushul. It was one of the routes the enemy was expected to attack from. The administrative base of C Company was about 10 km from battalion HQ and it took Maj Shaitan Singh and his company of 124 men three hours to climb to the pass. They took their heavy loads on yaks and ponies hired from local Ladakhis. Most of the men were from Haryana and had never seen snow before. Now, quite suddenly, they found themselves in freezing temperatures at a height of 16,420 feet. They had been moved from Baramulla, Jammu and Kashmir, and had hardly had time to acclimatize.

Maj Shaitan Singh placed his men on the forward slopes of the hill—Number 7 Platoon, under Jemadar Surja Singh, was on the north flank; 8 Platoon, under Jemadar Hari Ram, was in the pass area; and the central post was held by 9 Platoon under Jemadar Ram Chander, with the company HQ next to it. The mortar section, under Naik Ram Kumar Yadav, was on the reverse slope.

As the men went about digging bunkers and building defences, using sandbags, all that they had to shelter from the harsh, cold winds were 40-pounder tents. Every platoon had about 25 men. Each of them was aware that the orders issued by the battalion commander on 24 October said that if the Chinese attacked all sub-units were to fight to the last man and the last round.

'The weather was terrible; we didn't have proper winter clothes or shoes. The jerseys, cotton trousers and light coat we were issued could hardly keep us warm in those freezing winds. The soldiers would get terrible headaches and nursing assistant

Dharam Pal Dahiya would rush from post to post doling out medicines,' recounts Ram Chander. The quiet and soft-spoken Maj Shaitan Singh, would rough it out with his men.

As radio operator, Ram Chander's job was to establish communication between the different platoons. 'When we were free we would sit together and listen to All India Radio. We would hear about posts that the Chinese were attacking and how they were massacring our men. Our blood would boil. We were itching to teach them a lesson. "Hamein mauka milega toh ham jam kar ladenge" (If we get the chance, we will give a very good fight), we would tell Sahab and he would just smile back,' he says.

The greatest disadvantage of Rezang La was that it was crested to Indian artillery fire and could not get any artillery support because of the ridges around it. The men of C Company were thus completely isolated and they were equipped with outmoded .303 single action rifles of World War II vintage while the Chinese had the latest automatics. They were also under orders to not patrol the international border so all their patrols were restricted to within 400 yards of their location.

The battle of Rezang La

18 November 1962 is a Sunday. It is colder than usual and snow falls lightly over Rezang La.

Around 3.30 a.m., the stillness of the early morning is pierced by the staccato sound of an LMG burst. Maj Shaitan Singh quickly asks Ram Chander to tune the radio set. Jemadar Hari Ram from 8 Platoon comes on air and says that the enemy has tried to attack their listening post with about ten men but were spotted. Number 8 Platoon has directed LMG fire at the Chinese soldiers climbing from the gullies and killed most of them, while the remaining have run away.

'Shabash! Chaukas rahiye,' (Bravo! Be vigilant) says the major. Suspecting there could be more enemy attacks he orders a patrol to check the gullies between 7 and 9 Platoons.

The patrol returns and reports that these gullies are swarming with Chinese. The LMGs and mortars are put in position. Jemadar Surja Ram, 7 Platoon, reports that around 400 enemy soldiers are climbing up to their post. 'We can see them clearly against the snow,' he tells his company commander.

Maj Shaitan Singh orders him to fire at them the moment they come within shooting range. When the enemy soldiers are 250 yards away, 7 Platoon opens fire. Their three LMGs blaze for four minutes. They report that the enemy attack has been repelled.

Just then, 8 Platoon reports that 800 enemy soldiers are coming up from the ridge near them. 'Aap Veer Ahir hain, poore josh se ladiye,' (You are a Brave Ahir, fight with full spirit) the major tells Jemadar Hari who bravely replies, 'Aap chinta hi mat kariye Sahab, ham ladenge' (Don't worry, Sir, we will fight).

The platoon opens fire and the attack is neutralized. Maj Shaitan Singh orders mortar fire into the gully; Jemadar Hari Ram advises: 'Sahab, don't fire any more into that nala; it is full of dead Chinese men.'

After all their frontal attacks fail, the Chinese quickly change their plan. Around 4.30 a.m., they begin to shell all the posts at the same time. From the blinds recovered later, it is evident

*that they use three types of mortars; 120 mm, 81 mm and 60
mm. To destroy bunkers, they use 75 mm and 57 mm recoilless
(RCL) guns that they have brought there on wheelbarrows. The
four-foot-deep craters found in solid rock indicate that that they
also use 132-mm rockets. 'It was such a massive attack that no
one could help anyone else,' says Ram Chander. 'We could not
hear each other over the din; shells just came and blew up our
bunkers. Of our main operators, one had his head and the other
his legs blown off. Wooden planks were reduced to matchwood
and sandbags to shreds of gunny. It was all over in 15 minutes
and there was a trail of death and devastation left.'*

When the bombing ceases, the men who survive see yaks and
horses on the ridgeline. Company Havaldar Major (CHM)
Harphul Singh initially thinks it is Alpha Company coming to
their aid, but when he looks through his binoculars he realizes
it's the Chinese bringing reinforcements to attack 8 Platoon. At
the same time, 7 Platoon reports that nearly 700 enemy soldiers
are climbing up to their post.

Maj Shaitan Singh, who has been hit by a shell and has his
left arm in a bandage, rushes from man to man instilling courage
in them. He asked injured jawans to get first aid and be ready to
fight. 'All our bunkers were destroyed, our men were injured and
dead, our ammunition was running out, many of the jawans
could not even cock their .303 rifles since their fingers had frozen
in the cold, but Maj Sahab did not lose his nerve. He stood there
calmly and directed the men, telling them to be brave and to
battle on,' remembers Ram Chander.

Nihal Singh is on the LMG at the company HQ with
his partner Ram Meher Singh. Ram Meher is hit by a shell
and collapses. Left alone in the trench with no means of

communicating with anyone, Nihal keeps firing till he is shot.
He manages to pull apart the pieces of his LMG so that it does
not fall into enemy hands. He has grenades but no strength in his
arms to pull out the pins and throw them. Finally, he is pulled
out of the trench by enemy soldiers and taken away.

Maj Shaitan Singh is on the ridge when a medium machine
gun-burst hits him in the stomach. It also burns down the radio
set with Ram Chander so they are now completely cut off from
everyone else. CHM Harphul Singh grabs an LMG and kills
the enemy soldier who has hit Maj Shaitan Singh. He is hit by
RCL fire and collapses. Breathing his last, he tells Ram Chander,
'Don't let Maj Sahab fall into the enemy's hands'.

Maj Shaitan Singh is losing blood and slipping in and out of
consciousness. He repeatedly tells Ram Chander to open his belt
since his stomach is hurting. Ram Chander puts his hand inside
his shirt to find his intestines spilling out. 'I didn't open his belt
because everything would have fallen out,' he says.

Ram Chander holds him in a tight embrace and rolls down
into the ravine with him. Then, carrying his company commander
on his back, he walks 800 metres and, stopping near a boulder,
lays down the major. He meets another soldier, who is injured
and bleeding. They get caught in enemy crossfire.

Realizing that his men will not have a chance to escape if
they have to carry him, Maj Shaitan Singh orders them to leave
him where he is and save their own lives. 'Go back and tell them
how we fought till the last. This is my company. I want to die
here. Yeh aapke liye aadesh hai,' (This is my order) he insists, his
breath coming in painful gasps.

It is 8.15 a.m. The snow is still falling and the sky is a dull
grey. Reluctantly, the soldiers leave. They find their way to the

quarter master's shed only to find it burning. It has been set on fire by their own men, who had received orders to destroy everything and come back to battalion HQ in Chushul. The survivors walk six miles to reach the battalion.

Meanwhile, Nihal escapes that night from enemy custody and manages to reach his post. He finds bodies scattered like rag dolls. Maj Shaitan Singh's tent lies shredded to bits. His friend Chiman has his head blown off. Mahender from Mandola village is dragging himself around, his legs crushed.

'Bhai mujhe bhi le chal (Buddy, take me along),' Mahender implores him, but Nihal tells him he is helpless since his own arms are useless.

'I couldn't help Mahender,' he says sadly.

'Theek hai bhai, phir tu nikal (Alright buddy, you carry on),' Mahender tells him and Nihal turns to find his way back to his battalion headquarter. He sees the enemy firing illumination rounds into the air to spot him, but his white parka blends in with the falling snow and he manages to climb down the ridge undetected.

When he is tired and lost, Tommy, a big local dog from a nearby village, who has been a routine visitor to their post for meat, finds him. Nihal follows the dog blindly, tripping and falling on the slope.

Many hours later, a soldier at the battalion HQ in Chushul, looking through his binoculars, finds a wounded man pulling himself through the snow. He is recognized as Nihal of C Company. Both his arms are hanging limply by his side, his uniform is blood-stained and tattered, he has lost a lot of blood and is weak from lack of food and water. Nihal is brought back quickly, fed halwa and tea and then sent to Jammu hospital for treatment.

He is one of the survivors of Rezang La; he recounts the brave tale of the handful of men who tried desperately to save their post from falling into enemy hands. He speaks of the 1310 dead enemy soldiers whose bodies were taken back by the Chinese. He says the Chinese got 25 trucks in which they loaded the bodies of their men.

After the ceasefire, Rezang La falls into no man's land, which means it is disputed and not to be occupied by either country. Maj Shaitan Singh and his men lie frozen there till a shepherd discovers their bodies three months later.

'It is a credit to Maj Shaitan Singh's courage, devotion to duty and leadership that his men fought so bravely till the end despite knowing that the odds were against them. They did this because he was the perfect leader, who inspired them with his own example,' says Brigadier (Retired) R.V. Jatar, who was commanding D Company during the '62 war. 'The written orders that all company commanders had received from the battalion commander during that war were that you will fight to the last man, the last round. Shaitan was the kind of man, who followed orders to the T.'

Jatar talks about Maj Shaitan Singh with a lot of affection. 'His name was Shaitan Singh, but he was one of the finest gentlemen I have ever come across. Gentle and shy otherwise, he proved that he was a lion in war. The jawans loved him,' he says. He remembers how Shaitan's company had won a defence preparedness competition at Baramulla just five months before the war. 'In Rezang La they had very limited material, they could not even build proper overhead covering since they didn't have tin sheds and their company was completely bombarded. They couldn't have saved themselves.' Jatar recounts a story about when Shaitan and another officer were in a train and they chanced upon an astrologer. Just for fun they asked him to read their palms. 'When the astrologer saw Shaitan's hand, he prophesized that he was headed for great glory. Maybe he saw death, but he did not mention that,' says Jatar.

Great glory did come to Maj Shaitan Singh in a war that is mostly remembered with shame. Every man of C Company who fought at Rezang La was a hero. The name of Maj Shaitan Singh, who inspired his men so much that they preferred death to surrender, will live forever in the pages of India's military history. His supreme courage, leadership and exemplary devotion to duty inspired his company to fight gallantly to the last man. For this act of undaunted courage in the face of the enemy, he was awarded with the Param Vir Chakra (posthumously).

Shaitan Singh was born on 1 December 1924 at Banasar village in Jodhpur district, Rajasthan. The village is now known as Shaitan Singh Nagar. He belonged to the Bhati clan of Rajputs. He was from an Army family and was greatly inspired by his father Lieutenant Colonel Hem Singh, who had served with the Jodhpur Lancers and been injured in France during World War I; he had been awarded the OBE for his bravery and devotion to duty.

Shaitan studied in the Rajput High School, Chopasni at Jodhpur. He was a quiet and soft-spoken boy and good at sports, particularly football. He went on to play for the forces and had even played the Durand Cup. After completing his graduation, he joined the Jodhpur Lancers (Horse Squadron) and when the State Forces merged with the Indian Army, he joined the Kumaon Regiment.

Army officers, who bring their families for a holiday to Pangong Tso, the brilliant blue lake in Ladakh, often continue to drive up the mud track to Chushul, racing the wild horses called kiangs and watching grazing herds of blue sheep, or napo. They startle marmots nibbling on strands of grass and continue driving over the rocky road till they reach the Rezang La memorial.

The memorial has been built on the site where the men of C Company were cremated. There, inscribed on a white marble block, are the names of the martyrs of Rezang La and the following lines by Lord Thomas Macaulay:

How can a man die better
Than facing fearful odds,
For the ashes of his fathers,
And the temples of his gods.

SECOND KASHMIR WAR
OF 1965

The 1965 conflict is also known as the Second Kashmir War. The First War was fought in 1947–48.

One of the repercussions of the setback in 1962 war was that Pakistan felt India was weak militarily and that the timing was perfect for another bid to take over Kashmir. The Indian morale was low after facing the adverses in Sino-Indian War; the economy was stumbling, Jawaharlal Nehru had died and the next Indian prime Minister, Lal Bahadur Shastri, did not have his predecessor's charisma. Pakistan, on the other hand, was confident with US aid at its disposal. This included 200 Patton tanks, two squadrons of bombers, four squadrons of Sabre jets and one squadron of Supersonic fighters. They launched an attack in the Rann of Kutch, to which India retaliated, but status quo was reverted to when a ceasefire agreement was signed.

In early August, Pakistan started working on creating an insurgency by stealthily pushing troops into Jammu and Kashmir. The operation was termed Operation Gibraltar. It was aimed at infiltrating forces into Jammu and Kashmir to precipitate an insurgency against Indian rule. Pakistan believed that the local Kashmiris did not want Indian rule and would join in the movement. A guerilla force of more than 25,000 men armed, trained and aided by Pakistan, crossed the Line of Control and entered Kashmir disguised as locals.

Pakistan craftily termed the unrest as uprisings against Indian rule and planned an attack on India. On 15 August the Indian Army jumped into the fray, destroyed the guerrilla bases and captured areas like Haji Pir. Pakistan made an attempt to capture Akhnoor but failed. On 6 September, the Indian Army crossed the International border and war was declared officially.

The most famous battle of 1965 was the battle of Asal Uttar, meaning Befitting Reply. A famous tank battle was fought in the Khem Karan sector, where Pakistan incurred heavy losses. As many as 75 Pakistani Patton tanks were destroyed or deserted, and the Indians collected these as war trophies. In fact, the place where they lay deserted was named Patton Nagar by the locals and was a symbol of Pakistan's humiliating defeat. This was the battle in which Company Quarter Master Abdul Hamid of 4 Grenadiers got his Param Vir Chakra posthumously.

The other famous tank battle was the Battle of Chawinda, where Lieutenant Colonel A.B. Tarapore of 17 Horse lost his life and was decorated with the Param Vir Chakra posthumously.

The war, which caused a heavy loss of life for both countries, ended on the intervention of the United Nations and the signing of the Tashkent declaration.

Abdul Hamid

It is March 2014. A dilapidated, old house stands in the middle of golden wheat fields that are ready to be harvested in Dhamupur village, district Ghazipur, Uttar Pradesh. Many years ago this was the place where Abdul Hamid sat with a sewing machine, stitching clothes for people, with the chatter of his children echoing through the house.

Now even his wife Rasoolan Bibi doesn't live here. The fields have been rented out for cultivation while Hamid's family has shifted three kilometres away, near Dhulapur Railway Station from where Jameel, Rasoolan Bibi's grandson, says, it is easier to commute and to get medicine for his grandmother. Jameel takes a local train to commute to Varanasi every day for work.

There are only two things that Ghazipur is famous for, he says: the opium factory and his grandfather. 'Vir Abdul

Hamid' (Abdul Hamid, the Brave) is a chapter that class six students read in their Hindi literature books. When Jameel was in school, he read it too, and says he felt very proud that it was his grandfather that the teacher was telling the boys about.

Dhulapur Railway station is the same from where Hamid caught the local train to Varanasi in 1965 to his unit. It was deployed in the Khem Karan sector. That evening had brought with it some bad omens, as Rasoolan likes to call them, and she had tried her best to discourage her husband from leaving. But he had shrugged it off with a half smile. For him, the Army had always come first.

Hamid presses his rolled-up bedding with his knee and knots the thick rope binding it together. He is giving it another tug to make the bed roll tighter when the rope suddenly snaps, leaving one half in his hand. The bedding unfolds, spilling the contents. Amongst these is a muffler that Rasoolan has bought for her husband from a fair in a nearby village. She is in tears. 'That is a bad omen,' she says, 'Don't go today.'

Hamid says he cannot stay back; he has to join his battalion as per the orders. Telling her not to worry, and 'Didn't I return safe from the '62 war?', he gets on with his packing.

A little later, he leaves the house accompanied by relatives, and his friend Bachu Singh carrying his trunk and holdall on a bicycle; the chain of the cycle breaks. The villagers take this to be another bad sign and try to convince him to stay back for the night and take another train the next morning.

But Hamid does not listen. By the time he finally reaches the station the train has left. Undeterred, Hamid says he shall wait for the night train. He tells his friends and family to return. That is the last they will see of him.

Khem Karan Sector
8 September 1965, 9 a.m.

The fields are rustling with sugar cane and even as Hamid sits in the passenger seat of his jeep, which has mounted on it a recoilless (RCL) gun, he can hear the wind. The jeep trundles over a narrow mud track ahead of Cheema village. Hamid knows Pakistan has launched an attack with a regiment of Patton tanks that has barged right into the forward position. He hears the rumble of armour first and then catches sight of a few tanks that are heading towards his battalion.

Taking cover behind the tall crop, Hamid points his gun in their direction and then waits. The Grenadiers hold their fire so as not to warn the enemy. Just as the tanks come within 30 yards, Hamid asks his loader to load the gun and shoot. He watches the shell go up and arch towards the first enemy tank. Even as he picks up his binoculars, he hears the blast. The tank is burning in front of his eyes.

Hamid and his men rejoice. 'Shabaash!', Bravo, he mouths and they exchange wide smiles. They spot the crew of the two following tanks dismount and run away. Hamid orders the driver to reverse and move.

Around 11.30 a.m., the battalion is subjected to heavy artillery shelling and then they hear the familiar rumble again.

Hamid whips out his binoculars. Three more tanks are heading in their direction. He positions his jeep in the midst of the field to hide it from view and, positioning his gun, waits. The moment the tank comes within shooting distance, he signals to the loader and watches the trajectory of the shell. It hits target and one more tank is burning in front of his eyes while the remaining two are again abandoned by the Pakistanis. By the end of the day, Hamid has destroyed two tanks while four have been abandoned.

Demands are now made on the engineers to lay out anti-tank mines in the area since that is where the enemy tanks are coming in from. They do the best they can under the time available. It is clear that the battalion is facing a brigade-level attack from the Pakistani armoured forces and all they have to fight them with are RCL guns. That doesn't bother the soldiers who in high spirits after their initial victories.

The next morning Hamid is back at his job and he destroys two more tanks with his RCL gun. The battalion also faces an air attack from Pakistani Sabre jets but these don't do much damage. By the end of the day, Hamid and his team have shot down two more tanks. It is a remarkable achievement.

That night Abdul Hamid sleeps well. He is happy with his achievement. His citation has been sent for a Param Vir Chakra (PVC). It credits him with the destruction of four tanks.

The next day Hamid shows up on the battlefield yet again. He will destroy three more tanks (according to Jameel, who has heard about the battle from a survivor, who died a few years back). This, however, will not get entered into his records since his citation has already been sent.

10 September 1965

4 Grenadiers comes under heavy enemy shelling. After that there is another assault by enemy tanks. They are moving in a formation of three. Hamid waits under cover of vegetation and when the first tank gets close, he blows it up, quickly asking his driver to move away. Just as they do, a tank shell drops and bursts at the very spot where they were a few minutes ago.

The brave Grenadiers have moved to another point behind a thicket from where they are training their gun on another Patton. They shoot it down as well. By now, the shelling has started. The enemy tanks have noticed the jeeps and they concentrate machine gunfire on them. Hamid is tricking them by constantly changing his position and by keeping his jeep camouflaged by the tall sugar cane crop. Another tank slowly lumbers towards him, but he does not have the time to move since they have both spotted each other. Both place each other in their sights and shoot. Both shells hit their targets. There is a loud blast, fire and smoke. Even as the tank is blown up, its shell hits the jeep. The impact flings it in the air. There are screams of pain, a lound crash and then complete silence intercepted only by the crackle of flames.

Abdul Hamid is dead. He has blown up a total of seven enemy tanks, even more than an armoured formation can hope for.

For his remarkable achievement, bravery and courage, Abdul Hamid is awarded the PVC posthumously. The battalion is awarded the Battle Honour of Asal Uttar and the Theatre Honour (Punjab). For first time in military history a battalion with only RCL guns at its disposal has fought off an armoured division.

Abdul Hamid was born on 1 July 1933 in Dhamupur village of district Ghazipur in Uttar Pradesh to Sakina Begum and Mohammad Usman, who had three more boys and two girls. Abdul's father was a tailor by profession and Abdul would often help him stitch clothes before he decided to join the Army.

He began his schooling at the Basic Primary School, Dhamupur, and passed his class eight from Junior High School, Deva. Nature's child, Abdul enjoyed wrestling, swimming, hunting and gatka, a kind of sword fighting. When just 14, he was married to Rasoolan Bibi, and they had five children, one daughter and four sons.

Abdul was a proud man. His grandson Jameel recounts an incident when Haseen Ahmed, the zamindar of a nearby village, who was a good marksman, offered big prize money to anyone who would shoot down a particular bird which Ahmed himself had not been able to do.

Abdul borrowed his friend Bachu's gun and shot the bird, but refused to go to the zamindar for the prize money. It was Bachu who went there instead and when the zamindar asked for Abdul to come collect the prize, Abdul refused, saying, 'I might be poor, but I don't go begging to people's houses.' The zamindar later had the prize money sent to his house.

Hamid was 20 years old when he was recruited at Varanasi into the Army. After undergoing his training at the Grenadiers Regimental Centre at Nasirabad, he was posted to 4 Grenadiers in 1955. Initially, he served in a rifle company and was then posted to a recoilless platoon. He fought in the '62 war in Thang La, then in the North-East Frontier Province, as part of the 7 Mountain Brigade, 4 Mountain

Division, and came back disappointed with the war. After ceasefire was declared his unit moved to Ambala where Abdul was appointed Company Quarter Master Havildar (CQMH) of an administration company.

When Pakistan attacked in the Rann of Kutch area in April 1965, 4 Grenadiers was ordered to move forward and to collect their 106 RCL guns from the nearest ordnance depot. Hamid was one of the non-commissioned instructors. Due to absence of anti-tank detachment commanders, he was told to take over an anti-tank detachment. A very good marksman and an expert anti-tank gunner with a new anti-tank gun at his disposal, he made a big difference to the outcome of the war.

Hamid died on 10 September 1965. Though his citation credits him with destroying four enemy tanks, according to officers serving in the unit at that time, he actually destroyed three more. Since his citation was sent on 9 September, it did not count the three tanks he destroyed the next day; he was killed in action during the last fight with the seventh tank.

NOTE

There is ambiguity about how many tanks Hamid destroyed. According to *War Despatches: Indo-Pak conflict 1965* by Lieutenant General Harbaksh Singh, Hamid spotted four tanks in a sugar cane field, heading towards his company. Hiding his jeep behind a mound, he shot three of them from point-blank range. He also managed to hit the fourth but was blown to bits when a 90 mm shell hit his jeep.

An interesting aside of the '65 war is that after the Battle of Asal Uttar, meaning befitting reply, where the Pakistani tank division was completely routed, the deserted and damaged Pakistani Patton tanks were collected as war trophies. As many as 70 of them lay dumped in a place called Bhikkiwind, which the locals began calling Patton Nagar! According to Gen Harbaksh's book, in three days of the war, 75 Pakistani tanks were destroyed or abandoned, including the entire tank fleet of 4 Cavalry, whose commanding officer, 12 officers and several other ranks surrendered on the morning of 11 September.

After the ceasefire there sprang up a tank cemetery at Bhikkiwind, where some 70 Pakistani tanks were collected and parked before evacuation. The locals' name for it, Patton Nagar, was a unique memorial to all those who fought and fell at Asal Uttar or survived the ordeal of that battlefield to fight another day. The Pattons were displayed for a while after which they were taken to different Army cantonments across the country to be displayed as war trophies.

Abdul Hamid's grandson Jameel helped fill the gaps in this story by narrating conversations he had had with his grandmother Mrs Rasoolan Abdul Hamid. Mrs Hamid can no longer hear properly.

Ardeshir Burzorji Tarapore

The first time her father did not come back home, leaving the family very worried, Lieutenant Colonel Adi Tarapore's daughter Zarine was just 15. She could feel her mother's anxiety from the way she paced up and down the house. And she kept doing that till he came back.

The second time Lt Col Tarapore did not come back home, well, he just never did. No amount of worrying or praying or pacing could bring him back this time because the 1965 war had claimed him.

Zarine Mahir Boyce is now in her 60s and it has been nearly fifty years since her father Param Vir Chakra (PVC) Lt Col Ardeshir Burzorji Tarapore, died but memories of him are still fresh in her mind. Sitting in her Pune house, she remembers the loving dad and the brave soldier that he was. Sometimes, a smile lights up her voice but sometimes her voice is tinged with sadness. It has been many years, she says, but it does seem like it happened just the other day.

January 1964, Babina

The time was 7.45 p.m. The sun had set and the lights had been switched on in the handsome residence of the Tarapores, who lived in the cantonment. Adi was the commanding officer (CO) of The Poona Horse and he wasn't back yet. Mrs Perin Tarapore was starting to get seriously worried because he had promised her he would be home much earlier. It was the birthday of a civilian guest, who was staying over with the Tarapores, and Adi had promised her that he would be back by 6 p.m. so that they could cut the cake. The cake sat on the dining table, the kids—Xerxes and Zarine—were getting impatient, but there was no sign of Adi.

At quarter to eight Mrs Tarapore was relieved to hear the sound of a vehicle in the driveway. It was her husband's jeep. When the jeep stopped at the porch and Adi got off, she was horrified to see him walk in with his uniform covered in slush. His driver and wireless operator were similarly covered in grime. The kids and the guests had also collected around him by then and Adi apologetically told the group that his jeep had got stuck in the Gurari Nala, a stream that then flowed outside Babina. His uniform was dirty because he had helped his men push it to get it out of the slush. The guest, who was quite enamoured of Adi's rank and status, expressed shock that despite being the CO of the regiment, Adi had to get into the water to push the jeep. The normally gentle and polite Adi stiffened at that and retorted: 'I am not made of sugar and salt that I'd get washed away. Anything my men do, I do with them.'

Zarine, was listening to her father. She would never forget his words or his love for his men. Adi was to spend just one more year with his family. In September 1965, during the biggest tank battle fought between India and Pakistan at Phillora in the Sialkot sector, an enemy shell would hit his tank. Adi would be standing in the cupola when the tank would erupt in flames consuming him and his intelligence officer. He would die a hero's death right there on the battlefield, to the shock of the men he loved so much. At that time his left arm was already in a sling from an earlier injury for which he had stubbornly refused to be evacuated. Before that he would have led his men right into Pakistan and his unit would have successfully captured Jassoran and Buttar Dograndi. For the valour displayed by him in this action, lasting six days, Lt Col Ardeshir Burzorji Tarapore, would be awarded with the highest war-time gallantry medal, PVC, posthumously.

A born soldier

Ardeshir Burzorji Tarapore, lovingly called Adi by his friends, was born on 18 August 1923 in Mumbai. It is believed that the family name Tarapore came from the village of Tarapore that was one of the 100 in the mansab (estate) awarded by

Shivaji to his ancestor, who was a leader under the Maratha ruler eight generations back. The mansab was given as an appreciation for his courage and loyalty and incidentally these were the very qualities evident in Adi also, right from the time when he was a little boy.

There is an interesting story about his childhood. Adi had an older sister and a younger brother. When he was six, he was once playing with his 10-year-old sister Yadgar in their backyard. The family cow broke loose and charged at Yadgar. While Yadgar screamed in terror, little Adi quickly reacted. Picking up a stick, he stepped in front of the cow and smacked it on the nose with it. The startled cow backed off and the two children went back to their game.

This quality of fearlessness remained with Adi even as he got older. In those days, Hyderabad was a separate state and though Adi had his heart set upon joining the armoured regiment after leaving school, he was commissioned into the 7th Hyderabad Infantry as a Second Lieutenant in January 1942. How he got the Lancers and then Poona Horse is another interesting story.

It happened quite by chance. Once, when his battalion was being inspected by Major General El Edroos, the commander-in-chief of the Hyderabad state forces, during routine grenade-throwing training, a young sepoy panicked and accidentally lobbed his grenade right into the throwing bay. Without a thought for his own safety, Adi immediately jumped in and, picking up the grenade, flung it away. The grenade burst as it left his hand, and flying shrapnel embedded in his chest, but there were no other casualties. Maj Gen El Edroos was very impressed with the young officer and, when Adi had recovered from his injuries, called him to his office to congratulate him. Adi requested him for a transfer to an armoured regiment, and the general had him posted to the 1st Hyderabad Imperial Service Lancers. And thus Adi's dream was fulfilled.

Controversy, however, continued to dog Adi. During World War II the 1st Hyderabad Lancers saw service in the Middle East and was commanded by a British officer, who was rude and often criticized the fighting capabilities of the 'natives' under his command. On one occasion he insulted the Nizam. Tarapore, who was present, took strong exception to this and boldly told his CO, 'You have insulted my country and my king, and I do not mean George VI.'

The incident created a furore. The regiment was put into isolation and all its ammunition withdrawn. The matter was finally settled after Maj Gen El Edroos visited General Montgomery and Adi's career saved.

Adi joins the Poona Horse

Tarapore was posted to the the Poona Horse, or 17 Horse, after the merger of the Hyderabad State with the Union of India. There he joined A Squadron (which was a Rajput squadron) and, despite being a non-Rajput, developed such a close rapport with the men, that he was jokingly given the unofficial designation of 'Colonel of A Squadron'.

Lt Col Shivraj Singh, who was a newly commissioned subaltern at Chatha Camp in Jammu when Tarapore first joined the regiment, has written about the day Tarapore joined.

'Sometime in late 1951, news was received that an officer, ex-Hyderabad Lancers, was being posted to the regiment; he would be on probation for two years and would be given a permanent commission in the Army, only if he was found fit for retention in service. One fine day, when the officers were all sipping beer under the shade of a mango tree near the mess hutment, a well-built young officer of medium height walked in along with the second-in-command (2-IC) and was introduced as Captain Ardeshir B. Tarapore. The officer was very neatly and correctly dressed in his olive green uniform. He appeared somewhat shy and reticent, but confident, and was very polite and correct in his manners and conduct.'

That was Tarapore and soon he would become the darling of the regiment. In fact, he would develop such strong loyalty to 17 Horse that he would even start growing the fearsome cavalier moustache, modelling it on senior squadron NCO (non-commissioned officer) Bahadur Singh's moustache, and he would proudly tell the other officers that he was just following the 'true A Squadron tradition'. Even when he commanded the regiment many years later, Tarapore continued to sport this impressive moustache. He was fond of saying that the commandant of The 17 Horse only looked like a commandant if he sported a cavalier moustache.

Tarapore idolized Napoleon, Lt Col Shivraj remembers. He read about Napoleon extensively, often quoted him, and even kept a bust of the great man on his desk. In fact, when he was in high spirits, Tarapore often tried to emulate Napoleon much to the delight of other officers. Once, in the mess after a number of 'Har Har Mahadevs' preceded everyone downing their drinks, spirits were quite high, and Tarapore, after a few whiskeys, suddenly declared that he was a reincarnation of Napoleon. To prove it he struck a hero-like pose but felt the impersonation was incomplete without the right headgear. His eyes soon rested on the large silver mess bowl filled with water and floating rose petals. Tarapore quickly picked it up and inverted it over his bald pate, to represent Napoleon's hat. He then stuck his right hand into the jacket of his mess dress and adopted a typical Napoleonic stance. He was thoroughly drenched but his spirits were not dampened at all. For his fellow officers it was wholesome entertainment.

Tarapore is remembered by all his men and officers for his fearlessness and for being a hands-on CO. No task was too small for him. He often surprised soldiers by personally helping them load ammunition on to tanks, something that most other officers did not do. Sowar Nathu Singh remembers the time when Centurion tanks had just been introduced to the regiment, and the one he was driving had started making a lot of noise making him wonder what was wrong. Suddenly he saw Tarapore Saab (Sahib), who had been watching from afar, sprinting up to him. Reaching the tank, Tarapore jumped up to the cupola and gently told Nathu, 'Baccha, raise kam karo' (Child, lower the raise [of the engine]). Tarapore had gone abroad, trained and brought back Centurion tanks to the unit and no one knew them better than him.

When he was not fooling around with the boys in the mess, Tarapore was a good, steady, regimental officer. What made him stand out was that not only could he take quick decisions, he could also pick unorthodox solutions when the occasion demanded it. In 1962, Tarapore was officiating as the commandant, when the regiment received orders to move to its operational location within 24 hours. If normal procedures were followed, there was no way the regiment could have got ready in time, so Tarapore ordered the security fencing around the quarter guard, the regimental stores and the ammunition dump to be broken. Vehicles were driven up to the stores and loaded, and the tanks taken right up to the ammunition bays and stowed with ammunition. The entire regiment worked through the night and was able to move on schedule. The military engineering services could go on raising damage reports, which could be sorted out later! That was the kind of casual confidence with which Tarapore led his regiment even when he came back to command the 17 Horse and take on the might of Pakistan three years later.

The Battle of Chawinda was part of the Sialkot Campaign in the Indo-Pakistan War of 1965. It was one of the largest tank battles in history since the Battle of Kursk in World War II. The aim of the attack was to seize the key Grand Trunk Road around Wazirabad and Jassoran, which would enable domination of Sialkot–Pasrur railway, thus completely cutting off the Pakistani supply line. The striking force of the Indian 1st Corps was the 1st Armoured Division supported by the 14th Infantry and 6th Mountain Divisions and Indian infantry seized the border area on 7 September.

Crossing the border

On 27 August 1965, war was declared. Maj Ajai Singh of 17 Horse, who was home on leave for his son's birth, got to know of it when his father-in-law told him that Prime Minister Lal Bahadur Shashtri was addressing the nation on the radio.

The 17 Horse was at Kapurthala when the war was declared. Officers on leave, like Maj Ajai Singh, located their regiment following what they heard from locals about the tank movement. When Maj Ajai Singh finally found his unit and his CO, they had reached a village ahead of Samba. 'The reality of that war was that there were no maps, no one knew where to go; we were just told to be ready to go whenever the orders came,' he remembers nostalgically. The orders finally came one night.

It had rained in the night and the fields were full of slush. It was a cold winter morning when school-going children and women on their way to fill water in Barkhania, a border village of Pakistan, were surprised to see green battle tanks splashing past. They stood and watched in awe waving to the men in dungarees, who were standing upright in open cupolas. Some called out to the soldiers, who smiled back at them, while others just gaped at the 45 monster machines rumbling past languidly, one behind the other.

What the Pakistani villagers did not know was that these were the feared Centurion tanks of 17 Horse. They had received orders in the night to cross the Indo-Pak border at first light and that was exactly what they were doing. Lt Col Tarapore had passed on strict instructions that civilians were not to be harmed. 'Our fight is with the Army. We shall not touch any innocent men, women or children,' was what he had said, his voice cracking on the wireless sets. All the men could hear it. And that was why the villagers had mistaken them for friendly Pakistani soldiers.

Till the night before, the men of 17 Horse had been waiting patiently in their tents, 8 km inside of the border. In the night they could not only hear, but also see the firing between the two clashing armies. Needless to say, they were raring to join the battle. When the orders finally came, the nervous tension of the wait was immediately relieved and the men started preparing for war in earnest. They would finally see some action.

The Battle of Chawinda

It was the first day of the battle of Chawinda. The regiment was deployed in Sialkot district of Pakistan's Punjab province. When Lt Col Tarapore called his second-in-command Maj N.S. Cheema (now Lt Gen [retd]) aside, the latter thought it was a regular war briefing that the CO wanted to give him. However, it seems that the colonel had had a premonition about his own death.

Maj Cheema was surprised when Lt Col Tarapore went on to give him detailed instructions on what do in case he was killed in battle. "'I must be cremated in the battlefield," he said. "My prayer book must be given to my mother; my gold chain to my wife; my ring to my daughter; my bracelet and pen to my son,"' Col Tarapore told (then) Maj Cheema, who later recounted this to *Sakal Times* in an interview. 'He paused and then added, "And, Niranjan, please tell my son Xerxes to join the army".' Five days later, on 16 September 1965, Tarapore was fatally wounded after being hit by an enemy artillery shell.

The biggest tank battle of the 1965 Indo-Pak War took place at Phillora in the Sialkot sector. During the southern thrust of the Indian Army on the Kaloi-Phillora axis, 17 Horse commanded by Lt Col Tarapore advanced on the right flank.

The battle for Phillora started on 10 September with the Indian troops launching a massive attack. On 11 September, the regiment was assigned the task of delivering the main armoured thrust for capturing Phillora. It decided upon launching a surprise attack on Phillora from the rear. The 1st Armoured Division, equipped with four armoured regiments, was on the offensive in the area. Unstopped by the enemy, the tanks just kept moving into Pakistan. 'At around 11 a.m. the first air attack came. Till then the buggers had had no idea that we were so much inside their country,' chuckles General Ajai Singh, who was a young major in the C Squadron of 17 Horse, which was leading. Pakistan surprised the advancing Army by sudden strafing though the air attacks did more damage to lorry and infantry columns and less to the tanks. The toll was heavy, however, Gen Ajai Singh remembers; the regiments 16 Cavalry and Hodson Horse were butchered. There was complete chaos. Many of the men standing in their cupolas were hit and just collapsed or were badly injured. Gen Ajai Singh remembers he was standing on his turret when a shell hit his toolbox and his blanket caught fire. The fire was quickly put out and no damages were incurred.

The Patton tanks of Pakistan were facing the armoured units 16 Cavalry and Hodson Horse. The air attack had taken such a heavy toll that they were reeling back. The morale of the men was at a low. It was at this time that, on Tarapore's initiative, 17 Horse moved in to stabilize the situation. As was typical of him, he did not wait for instructions and just attacked the Pakistanis without any warning. 'And what a ferocious attack it was,' says the old General remembering that smoke-filled morning with pride. 'We destroyed 13 tanks in the first go.' Intense fighting continued for two days and Pakistani forces were forced to beat a retreat towards Chawinda. Phillora was captured by the Indians 3.30 p.m. on 11 September. Pakistan's 11 Cavalry fought well, but lost so many tanks that from that day onwards it ceased to function as a complete tank regiment. Tarapore was wounded in the operation. A splinter had smashed through his arm leaving a gaping wound. Since he was not able to move his arm, it had to be put in a sling.

After the capture of Phillora, the brigade commander and general officer commanding came over to compliment 17 Horse. Immediate awards were discussed but Lt Col Tarapore brushed them off saying his regiment was just doing its duty. He refused to be evacuated insisting that the wound was 'just a scratch'. Besides, he still had to oversee the attack on Chawinda. Meanwhile the Pakistani forces retreated and regrouped. They would put up a last fight at Chawinda.

The capture of Buttar Dograndi

The plan was that Chawinda would be attacked by the infantry on the afternoon of 13–14 September and 17 Horse would encircle it. The task was given to C Squadron. Gen Ajai Singh remembers how his squadron's tanks started moving in with

9 Garhwal as support. The Indian Army did not realize that Pakistani tanks were already hiding under cover in Buttar Dograndi, waiting for the attack. When C Squadron's tanks broke cover to attack the village, six out of ten were shot on the spot by the Pakistani Pattons. Since the enemy was hidden and the 17 Horse tanks had to move out of the sugar cane fields and expose themselves for the attack, the situation quickly took a turn for the worse. Maj Ajai Singh immediately called his CO on the wireless and informed him about the situation.

'I asked him for immediate reinforcements otherwise Buttar Dograndi would be lost.' He recollects how Tarapore moved in at once with his own tank while directing A Squadron to join the battle as well. 'I don't know if the message got relayed properly or not in the complete chaos of war but when the others saw the CO's tank moving towards Buttar Dograndi, some started following him as well. The result was that I had reinforcements.' says Gen Ajai Singh.

While the Pakistani Pattons were well-hidden in the foliage in the village a km away, the Indian tanks had broken cover from sugar cane fields for the attack. It was a daring attack, but the nine Centurions— which included five of Maj Ajai Singh, three of A Squadron and one of CO Tarapore—attacked the Pattons and destroyed all six of them. Buttar Dograndi was captured.

It was a moment of silent celebration for 17 Horse and its CO. Not only had Lt Col Tarapore defied the enemy's charge, he had held his ground and gallantly attacked Phillora. Though under continuous enemy tank and artillery fire, he had remained unperturbed throughout this action. When wounded, he had refused to be evacuated.

On 14 September, he again led his regiment to capture Wazirwali. Unmindful of his injury, he captured Jassoran and Buttar Dograndi on 16 September. In this battle his own tank was hit several times. But despite the odds, he maintained his pivots at both these places and thereby helped the supporting infantry to attack Chawinda from the rear. Inspired by his leadership, the regiment fiercely attacked and destroyed approximately 60 enemy tanks, suffering only nine tank casualties.

The valour displayed by him in this action, lasting six days, was in keeping with the highest traditions of the Indian Army. But soon, he would meet a painful though glorious end.

The last day

Tarapore is quite relaxed. He has finished his prayers in a relaxed way, the daring capture of Buttar Dograndi is fresh in his mind and he is proud of the men he has commanded. The battle is still on, but he knows it is just a matter of time before Pakistan caves in. Standing at his tank hatch, he is watching the battlefield, a cup of tea in his right hand, the left arm still in a sling. He is discussing the situation with his intelligence officer who is also on the tank and standing to his right. It is typical of him to stand in the open, unguarded, giving instructions or just surveying the area. At that unfortunate moment, a freak shell whizzes in and hits his tank, setting it on fire at once. Both Tarapore and his intelligence officer are enveloped in flames. They have taken a direct hit.

Maj Ajai Singh is evacuating a gunner who has fallen off his tank, and he freezes when he hears from his operator that the CO has been hit. Shocked, he rushes to the spot to find Lt Col Tarapore's lifeless body laid out on the ground, bathed by the orange rays of the setting sun.

It is 6 p.m. While Lt Col Tarapore's body is tearfully taken back, his disabled tank Khushab, named after a famous battle honour where the 17 Horse got two Victoria Crosses, has to be left behind. It is later captured by Pakistan.

For the valour displayed by him in this action, lasting six days, which is in keeping with the highest traditions of the Indian Army, Lt Col Ardeshir Burzorji Tarapore is decorated with the highest war-time gallantry medal, the Param Vir Chakra, posthumously.

NOTE

The continued thrust by the Indian Army into Pakistani territory finally culminated in the Battle of Chawinda, where the Indian Army's advance was halted. On 22 September, the United Nations Security Council unanimously passed a resolution that called for an unconditional ceasefire by both nations. With the signing of the ceasefire, all offensives were ceased on that front. The war ended the following day. India still retained almost 518 sq. km of Pakistan territory in the Sialkot sector, including the villages of Phillora, Pagowal, Maharajke, Gadgor and Bajagrahi, which were returned to Pakistan after the Tashkent Declaration.

With two Victoria Crosses and two PVCs—2nd Lt Arun Khetarpal and Lt Col Adi Tarapore—on its honour rolls, the Poona Horse remains the most decorated unit of the Indian Army.

THE INDO–PAK WAR
OF 1971

The Indo-Pak War of 1971 was brought on by the Bangladesh's struggle for independence.

In 1970, elections were held in Pakistan. The Awami League won 167 out of 169 seats in East Pakistan and a simple majority in the 313-seat lower house of the Parliament of Pakistan. However when Sheikh Mujibur Rahman staked claims to forming the government, then West Pakistan's Pakistan People's Party (PPP) leader Zulfikar Ali Bhutto refused to yield the prime ministership to him and President Yahya Khan called the military to crush the resulting protests in East Pakistan.

In April, exiled Awami League leaders formed a government-in-exile. Lieutenant General Tikka Khan, infamously called the Butcher of Bangladesh, let loose a reign of terror in which the armed forces used machine guns, tanks and artillery against unarmed civilians and Bengali paramilitary forces. This resulted in a mass exodus of scared civilians, who started crossing the border and, fearing for their lives, became refugees in India. It is believed that politically the war started in April, when Pakistan unleashed a wave of terror, rape and murder, pushing around nine million refugees into India.

The Indian government repeatedly implored the international community to intervene and resolve the crisis, but that did not happen. The thousands of refugees put a big strain on India's economy and also caused law and order problems. The crisis was completely ignored by the rest of the world and finally Prime Minister Indira Gandhi decided that armed action would have to be taken against Pakistan.

India waited for the winter when snowfall would close the Himalayan passes, making Chinese intervention difficuLt On the evening of 3 December, the Pakistani Air Force launched a pre-emptive strike on eleven airfields in India, including Agra. It had hoped that by escalating the crisis, it would make China and the US join in and then there would be a UN intervention. It did not factor in the alacrity with which the Indian forces would respond.

That evening, Indira Gandhi announced on radio that the air strikes were a declaration of war by Pakistan and the Indians would retaliate. The planning and conduct of this war was exemplary. The Indian Air Force achieved commendable success by dominating the Eastern theatre of war completely within 48 hours. This enabled the advancing army columns to move without any fear of detection even in daytime.

Abled by great planners and effected by inspired troops, the retaliation was quick and decisive. Within 15 days the war was over, more than 90,000 prisoners of war were taken, Pakistan suffered a crushing defeat and Bangladesh won its independence. The Instrument of Surrender of Pakistani forces stationed in East Pakistan was signed in Dhaka on 16 December 1971.

The well-recognized picture which hangs in many Army establishments shows General Officer Commanding-in-Chief of Eastern Command of the Indian Army Lt General Jagjit

Singh Aurora and Commander of Pakistani forces in East Pakistan Lt Gen A.A.K. Niazi.

The war was fought in two sectors—the Eastern and the Western. Many tales of supreme bravery emerged from this war. Four Param Vir Chakras were awarded to brave hearts Lance Naik Elbert Ekka of 14 Guards, Major Hoshiar Singh of 3 Grenadiers, Second Lieutenant Arun Khetarpal of 17 Horse and Flying Officer Nirmal Jit Singh Sekhon of the Air Force. Sekhon remains the only Air Force officer to get the Param Vir Chakra.

Only one recipient—Maj Hoshiar Singh—survived to tell his tale.

Albert Ekka

A man is crouched motionlessly on the ground; around him are nasty swamp bubbles. His boots are caked with dried mud, and he can feel an ant crawl across his left leg. He does not move an inch; ants are the least of his worries. Something drips down his neck and instinctively he touches it. It feels too sticky to be sweat. Lance Naik Albert Ekka brings his hand forward. It is too dark to see but he isn't surprised to smell blood. Wiping his palm on his pants, he grips his gun again.

It is going to be first light soon. Ekka can tell this even before he notices the faint orange glow seeping through the purple sheen of the night up in the east. He is an adivasi and knows these things instinctively, as do most tribals. The stars are still in the sky when he drops to his knees and goes into a snake crawl with his 7.62 rifle in his hands.

The bullet lodged in his arm sends a shooting pain down his arm. Another has caught him in the neck, making him stagger and fall before he grits his teeth and picks himself up again. A thin trickle of blood is oozing from the gaping hole and curving right down to his collar and into his neck. This wound is still warm and isn't hurting just yet but he knows it is just a matter of time before the blood loss and the pain gets him. Ignoring it for the time being, he put his weight forward on his elbows and crawls into the darkness making his way to the old double-storied railway signal building from where the enemy medium machine gun (MMG) fire is coming.

When Lance Naik Albert Ekka reaches the building where the enemy soldiers have made a bunker, he can hear the deadly rattle of the machine gun booming in his ear. The ground trembles under his feet each time the gun goes off, filling the night with cries of his own men, helpless before its killer accuracy and range. The guns his own troops have are no match for the powerful MMG fire. If this operation is to be successful the enemy MMG has to be silenced.

Slinging his rifle on his back, Ekka reaches for the grenade on his beLt Removing the pin with his teeth and spitting it out in one quick move, he lobs it inside the old brick structure through a gap. He then waits for the soft hiss to die down.

Before the two men inside can realize what has happened, the grenade has exploded, making Ekka squint in the sudden light and recoil from the splinters that hit him in the stomach. It throws one soldier against a wall with its force, reducing him to a mass of flesh and blood. The other is unharmed and still bent over the MMG.

Ekka climbs up the rusty old iron ladder leaning against the building and jumps in from a window. He takes his rifle off his shoulder and with the gleaming blade of the bayonet charges at the soldier operating the machine gun. Ghonp-nikal, ghonp-nikal: he remembers the ustad's instructions clearly. It has been hardly four years since his training and he has always been a quiet, but good student, silently absorbing lessons.

The time has come to put what was taught to test. Screaming with cold fury, Ekka charges at the machine gun operator and just as he turns around pushes the bayonet right into his stomach. Pulling it out with all his might, he raises his rifle and plunges the blade back into the man's chest. Again. And again.

The MMG is still smoking when its operator drops down in a bloody pile. Ekka wipes the dead man's blood off his face and stands there with the bloodied bayonet in his hands. His eyes bear a look of quiet satisfaction. And extreme exhaustion.

The machine gun has fallen silent. Everything is at a standstill. The night is suddenly quiet.

And then the battle turns in favour of the Indian soldiers. Major O.P. Kohli, company commander, Bravo Company, who is just 10 feet away directing the other men, has watched Ekka lob the grenade and climb into the signal station. Through the cracks in the building he can see Ekka attack the gunner and then turn. His heart fills with pride at what his man has done and he watches the building, waiting for Ekka to show up at the window.

He is relieved to find the small, slim soldier climb out and

step on the iron ladder to join the rest of the men. With bated
breath, he watches Ekka start to climb down. And then suddenly,
Ekka's body goes limp and he collapses and falls off the ladder.

Lance Naik Albert Ekka is dead. He has succumbed to his
injuries. But he has accomplished his mission. While the men of
Bravo Company go about clearing bunkers, free of the MMG
that has been stalling their attack, Lance Naik Albert Ekka lies
dead under the iron ladder that leads to the old brick signal
station of Gangasagar.

The sun slowly appears from behind the darkness. The stars
disappear one by one and soon it is dawn.

Camp Abrera, On The Banks of Chambal
February 1968

Lieutenant O.P. Kohli, of Bravo Company, 32 Guards (later
renamed 14 Guards) Insurgency Unit, was at Abrera camp
on the banks of the Chambal River, about 30 km from
Kota, when a thin and dark young boy called Albert Ekka
was marched up to him. He had cleared his battle physical
efficiency test (BPET) and was now standing before Lt Kohli
expressionlessly, refusing to meet his eyes.

Lt Kohli nodded at the newcomer and asked for him to
be added to the rolls. Ever since the new battalion had been
raised on 13 January 1968, it had been receiving men from
the Sikh Light Infantry, Bihar, Kumaon and the Guards.
Albert had come from a Bihar regiment. 'Frankly, I wasn't
much impressed by the unassuming, docile and quiet young

man. But he was an adivasi so I knew he would be physically fit and that was all we needed,' remembers Colonel Kohli, Sena Medal, retired now and heading the Delhi regional office of an ATM security agency. Sitting in his conference room with a cup of tea in his hand, he smiles gently, recounting the memories that are streaming in. 'We were together in the war. I was his company commander. But really, looking at him then, no one could have guessed what glory Albert was going to bring us.'

In May 1968, 32 Guards (I) was moved to Mizoram. Ekka was now section commander even though he was still a lance naik (normally a naik is the section commander). He was slowly coming into his own. He took part in counter insurgency operations, and showed great innovation. He was good with his subordinates and instilled respect. 'His command and control were good particularly because he was very reserved and did not mix with others or speak much. His face would always remain blank and he would talk only on a need-to-know basis. One could never tell from his face if he was happy or sad, and what he was thinking,' remembers Col Kohli.

He also remembers how Albert was completely disinterested in his personal appearance or his uniform. He would wear whatever size of uniform was issued to him without bothering to get it fitted by a tailor. The result was that his clothes hung limply on his thin frame and invoked the ire of his company commander, who was a bit of a stickler for smart turnouts. 'I would often pull his belt which would be hanging at his waist and tell him to smarten up his appearance,' Col Kohli smiles. However, Ekka made up for his disinterest in the way he looked with his killer instincts in the wild. When the company was out on a patrol, he would spice up meals by catching crabs in the nullah, roasting them on fire and serving them sprinkled with salt and chilli powder to the men. He was good at firing and excellent at setting traps for birds and wild boar. Often he would take his gun and a round of ammunition and come back from the jungle with a catch. And then when the time came for battle, he proved himself there gloriously too.

The trouble started in March 1971, when 32 Guards was in Dimagiri, and the refugees started entering India in hordes. Everybody could sense that it was just a matter of time before war was declared. Nine months passed and finally the orders came in December.

Gangasagar, Eastern front, Bangladesh Liberation War
Night of 3 December 1971

The Alpha and Bravo Companies were told to attack Gangasagar railway station, which the enemy had converted into a virtual fortress by establishing bunkers all around. The C Company was moved out to create a diversion while the D Company stayed with the battalion headquarters. The artillery was kept on call but not brought into action since the aim was to surprise the enemy by moving into their defences silently and the big guns would have alerted them.

It was 2 a.m. when the men of Alpha and Bravo Companies

started their march into enemy territory. Since the general area was marshy and a soldier walking there could easily sink up to his knees in the slush, the men were asked to walk in single file along the railway track that had been laid on an embankment 8–10 feet high and equally wide. Enemy soldiers had earlier been observed walking along the track so the guards knew that the area was not mined.

As per plan, Alpha Company started walking along the right of the track and Bravo on the left. The men were moving quietly in the night, one behind the other. To maintain coordination between the two marching companies, Lance Naik Gulab Singh and Lance Naik Ekka were appointed as guides to march on top of the embankment, one on either side guiding their respective companies from the height. The orders were that the men would move along the railway track and charge when they saw the enemy. B Company Commander Maj Kohli (he had been promoted) was walking down below along the railway track with the troops. He could see Ekka right above, his thin frame a dark shadow moving silently in the night. This was how the two companies marched on, one on either side of the railway track with the two guides moving together on top, till they reached the enemy position.

All was going well till one of the guides walked into a trip-flare wire that the enemy soldiers had laid out across the railway line. The moment the device went off, it sent a bouquet of fireworks into the air, illuminating the area like daylight. The two men on top stood exposed. Just 40 yards away from where Ekka was standing was an enemy bunker with a sentry on duty outside.

Startled by the noise and light, the soldier on sentry duty

shouted: 'Kaun hai wahan?' (Who goes there?) It was 2.30 a.m. and he was still trying to figure out if the trip wire had been set off by a man or an animal.

'Tera baap,' (your father) replied Ekka and charging ferociously with his gun he bayoneted the enemy soldier.

There were four men, a light machine gun (LMG) and a recoilless (RCL) gun in that first bunker they encountered. Ekka was shot in the arm but the bunker was quickly taken over.

Thereafter, all hell broke loose. Pakistani troops started lighting up the area, firing illumination rounds. LMG and MMG fire was directed at the two attacking companies. The night rang out with the sound of gunfire and cries of men attacking each other. There was a pond behind the railway station with a bandh (dam) around it and the enemy soldiers had fortified the entire area with numerous bunkers. A and B Companies, with 120 men each, split up here. While A Company moved straight down, B Company moved around the pond, from one enemy bunker to another. Molotov Cocktails were charged and activated. Flinging them at the enemy soldiers the two companies moved on with complete disregard for their personal safety. They went from bunker to bunker, assaulting armed soldiers and taking over the enemy positions. The single aim was to kill enemy soldiers and clear the bunkers.

Despite the bullet in his arm Ekka was charging like a lion. He was walking alongside Maj Kohli when another bullet hit him in the neck.

Kohli watched him stagger and fall. 'But then, he quickly picked himself up, stood tall and kept walking,' he recounts.

By then, the men had reached the railway signal building from where the MMG was firing continuously. It was a big hindrance to the soldiers. There was a need to silence the deadly machine gun. This was exactly where Ekka would perform his supreme act of bravery.

———

In the battle of Gangasagar, 11 soldiers lost their lives while one officer, three junior commissioned officers (JCOs) and 55 other ranks were seriously injured. Twenty-five enemy soldiers were killed while six were taken prisoners of war. The battalion was awarded three Sena Medals, one Vir Chakra and one Param Vir Chakra (PVC) for the bravery of its men.

Besides Ekka's brave feat, that got him his PVC posthumously, there were many individual acts of sacrifice and cold courage that made highlights in the Battle of Gangasagar. Tilak Ram of RCL platoon managed to pinpoint the position of the enemy RCL gun and, unmindful of his own safety, jumped on the enemy, killing two soldiers on the spot. For his act of bravery, Tilak Ram was awarded a Sena Medal. Young artillery officer Captain K. Mahadevan, who was providing fire support to his own troops, was repeatedly exposed to enemy fire but refused to move and kept directing artillery fire to support the Indian troops. He was also decorated with a Sena Medal.

The advance along the railway line was also subjected to heavy fire. Major Tara, the right forward company commander, did not think twice before rushing to the enemy MMG and, flinging a Molotov cocktail and grenade at the bunker, pulled the gun out. This daring action brought him a Vir Chakra.

The PVC given to Ekka was even more special for all concerned with the action because it was the first to come to Bihar and also the first won by the brigade of the Guards. It was the only PVC awarded in the Eastern Theatre as well.

———

Lance Naik Albert Ekka was the son of Julius and Mariam Ekka. Born and brought up in a village in Bihar, he came from an adivasi tribe in Ranchi and was a devout Christian. From the time when he was a little boy Albert was fond of hunting and like all adivasis was an expert at tracking and hunting animals, often using his bow and arrow. He was also good at games. His love for adventure and his hunting skills made him an excellent soldier. When Albert grew up he was very keen to join the Army since it appealed to his sense of adventure and action.

Nirmal Jit Singh Sekhon

Srinagar
14 December 1971

It is another freezing morning at the Srinagar air force base. And who would know the bone-chilling cold better than the 26-year-old, tall and lanky Flying Officer Nirmal Jit Singh Sekhon, with the crisp upturned moustache, and Flight Lieutenant Baldhir Singh Ghuman, both of whom have got there at 4.30 a.m. in a bus with most of its windowpanes missing. The 45-minute ride from Badami Bagh officers' mess, where they live in dingy, dimly lit rooms, to the airbase has made their teeth chatter and nearly frozen their joints but for the pilots of 18 Squadron (Flying Bullets), this is routine. Those on morning shift have to get to the base and be battle ready at least half-hour before daylight. Pilots on two-minute standby have to remain strapped to their seats in the cockpit of their parked planes but since it is extremely cold, they are relieved after every three hours.

The two young officers are sitting in the small, cramped aircrew room, 30 m from where their Gnats are parked in the open, though neatly camouflaged, pens. Since it has been a particularly foggy morning with very low flight visibility, they have been taken off the two-minute standby, but are still on air defence alert and a five-minute standby, which means they should be able to get airborne in five minutes.

Both are from the 18 Squadron, which has been stationed at Ambala but is now more at Srinagar since March 1971 after tensions have escalated between India and Pakistan. Until now, the Indian Air Force has been following UN restrictions of no combat aircraft in Jammu and Kashmir. Neither Sekhon nor Ghuman are new to Kashmir's terrain and weather and both are fully confident since they have complete faith in the Gnats they fly. The tiny planes have been termed Sabre Slayers after their phenomenal performance in the '65 war when they held their own against the larger Pakistani Sabre jets, shooting down as many as seven of them.

Suddenly, an alarm is sounded from Awantipur Airbase. Pakistani Sabre jets are headed towards Srinagar. Since the base does not have air defence radar and visibility is also low, it is very difficult to spot enemy planes till they are very close. A chain of observation posts has been set up along the hill crest in the west where a soldier from the local regiment is put on duty. He has a battery-operated radio set and his task is to report immediately if he spots enemy aircraft in the air.

The two fighter pilots are told to be on Standby 2. They run out of the aircrew room and make a dash for the pens where their *faithful Gnats are standing. Clipping on his helmet, Sekhon, called Brother by his friends, climbs into his Gnat. Ghuman, popularly called G'Man, makes a dash for his own plane. Both are in high spirits. It is every pilot's desire to get a slice of action and it looks like the dream is about to come true for the two of them today.*

Earlier that day, in Pakistan

A formation of four plus two F 86 Sabres of Pakistan Air Force's 26 Squadron (Black Spiders) takes off from Peshawar air force base and heads towards Kashmir. Their orders are to dive into the Kashmir Valley, bomb Srinagar, turn and get back to Pakistan. Each is carrying two 500-pound bombs and is ready for attack. All six Sabres also carry external 760 litre fuel tanks to stretch their endurance. While four of them are on the bombing mission, the other two are escorting them to facilitate the attack. Both have six fully loaded M3 Browning machine guns.

The 14 December strafing of Srinagar airbase was not the first time that the beautiful city had been bombed by Pakistan air force planes. In the 1971 War, the Srinagar airfield was subjected to 14 such daylight attacks. According to Air Commodore (retd) Ramesh V. Phadke, who was Sekhon's course mate and also posted in Srinagar in the same squadron during the war, the reason for this was not just the easy access

Pakistan had to the Valley, but also the fact that they had stationed an intelligence agent in Srinagar, who would warn them if the deadly Gnats were in the air. On more than two occasions, the enemy planes had retreated from the Pir Panjal Pass because they had received information that the dreaded Sabre Slayers were in the air, he says.

———

On this morning, the Sabres cross Pakistan and enter India by flying over the Pir Panjal range at 10,000 feet. They are spotted when they cross Awantipur air force base, and an alarm is immediately raised. At the Srinagar Airbase, Sekhon and Ghuman have started their Gnats. The airbase has a 3,500-yard runway, a parallel taxi track and a few airplane shelters made of concrete, called blast pens, right at the end of the runway where four Gnats are usually stationed at a time. The two fighter pilots are impatiently waiting for clearance from the air traffic control, which is a dug-out on the eastern side of the runway. The din of the approaching planes is getting closer every moment and now reverberating in their ears. Ghuman decides not to wait any more and takes off. By then the Sabres are overhead and two of them have dropped lower and are strafing the airstrip.

Ignoring the risk to his own life, Sekhon, who has been waiting for the runway to clear, lifts off in another 20 seconds. Even as the two Sabres drop their bombs on the air strip, his Gnat lifts gracefully into the air. Beneath him the air strip is covered with smoking potholes. Above him, somewhere in the fog, is Ghuman. Ideally, the scramble or the order for takeoff should have been cancelled since the enemy aircraft were overhead and had already

*begun bombing the runway, but this does not concern Sekhon,
who smiles to himself and pulls the joystick. He doesn't know
then that this is the last time he and Ghuman will fly together.*

---

*Once in the air, Sekhon immediately lines up behind the two
Sabres that are regrouping after their bomb run and starts chasing
them. Ghuman is lost in the fog. They have lost each other and
will not reconnect. Ghuman will land back on the bombed
airstrip, half an hour after the air battle is over. After a fierce
and daring fight at treetop height, the completely outnumbered
Sekhon would have crashed in the valley by then, his parachute
only half deployed.*

*The moment the Sabres realize they are being chased by the
tiny though lethal Gnat, they take a sharp left turn. High on
adrenaline, Sekhon turns with them and fearlessly follows. His
voice crackles over the radio set: 'I am behind two Sabres. I
won't let the bastards get away.' Meanwhile, Sabre nos 3 and 4
have also dropped their bombs and are pulling up. While Sabre
no. 3 spots the dogfight and joins up with the two Sabres Sekhon
is chasing, Sabre no. 4, possibly waylaid by the fog, turns back
towards Pakistan. Sekhon positions himself behind Sabre no. 2
and opens fire with his 30-mm gun. The familiar gunfire is heard
at the airbase. A plume of fire and smoke is seen rising from the
Sabre. Flight Lieutenants Bopaya and Naliyan of 18 Squadron
later verify seeing a Sabre with its right wing on fire. Pakistan
denies any hit.*

*Sekhon revs up his engines and now decides to go after Sabre
no. 1. Sabre no. 3 has, however, closed the gap and Sekhon is*

sandwiched between the two large planes with the one behind shooting at him. The three get locked in a fierce dogfight. 'I'm in a circle of joy, but with two Sabres. I am getting behind one, but the other is getting an edge on me,' Sekhon's voice is heard on the radio.

None of the action is visible to onlookers from the airfield. The Sabre behind Sekhon continuously spews out a stream of 0.5" bullets, but he dodges them efficiently and continues to trail the Sabre in front. The third Sabre shoots his gun empty and fails to get a hit. The Pakistanis are shocked when the pilot's voice crackles on the radio: 'Three is Winchester,' meaning he has finished 1,800 rounds and his guns cannot fire any more.

Ammunition finished, Sekhon drops out of the fight and is now free of its threat. He uses this moment of temporary relief to straighten and drop his external fuel tanks so that he is much lighter and more agile. He goes after Sabre no. 1 with renewed enthusiasm. Nimbler than before, he starts making even tighter turns. The Sabre tries its best to lose the Gnat on its tail, but Sekhon closes in and after he gets the Sabre in his shooting range, starts firing at it with his 30-mm cannon. The Sabre gives up and makes an SOS call for help.

Sekhon is completely unaware that the formation of attacking Sabres actually has six and not four planes and that the two escorts are watching the fight from a distance, astonished by the dexterity with which the Gnat is turning and holding the big Sabre prisoner. On hearing the SOS call they dive down. Gaining a speed advantage from its dive, one of the Sabres closes in on Sekhon. Sekhon spots the two newcomers and realizes he is outnumbered. The rear Sabre fixes the Gnat with his machine gun and makes a continuous attack. The Gnat gets the bullets.

'I think I have been hit, G'Man come and get them,' is Sekhon's last message. Trailing smoke and fire, the tiny Gnat tries to steady itself, but continues to lose height and snaps over backwards. It nosedives and corkscrews into a gorge near Badgam. Sekhon tries to save himself by ejecting but he is too low and his parachute does not deploy properly. He crashes. Ghuman lands on the badly bombed runway half an hour later.

When the crashed Gnat is finally found, it has 37 bullet holes around the rear fuselage, tail plane and fin. It has however singlehandedly sabotaged the attack by six Sabres, which is a remarkable achievement.

For his exemplary courage and heroism in the Indo-Pakistan War of 1971, Flying Officer Sekhon is posthumously awarded the Param Vir Chakra. He remains the only Air Force personnel to be awarded the country's highest gallantry award.

Nirmal Jit Singh Sekhon was born in RurkaIsewal village of Ludhiana, Punjab, on 17 July 1945. He was the son of Warrant Officer Trilok Singh Sekhon, which made him a second-generation officer of the Indian Air Force.

Sekhon was commissioned into the Air Force on 4 June 1967. He was from the 97 GD (P) Pilots' Course and was posted to No. 18 Squadron (Flying Bullets) in October 1968. He was a brave though unassuming man with a lot of experience in flying Gnats. More than six feet tall, Sekhon was lanky with an awkward gait and people sometimes wondered how he could fit into the cockpit of the tiny Gnat. He was a simple man from a rustic background and was affectionately called 'Brother' by his course mates and friends because of his habit of starting all conversations with the word 'Brother', a literal translation of the word 'bhai' that he probably used in his village.

He was twenty-six years old when he died and had been married for just a few months, most of which he had spent on duty in Srinagar. He was awarded the Param Vir Chakra for his heroic action during the bombing of Srinagar airbase by Pakistan. The young and fragile Mrs Sekhon, draped in a white shawl, receiving the PVC from President V.V. Giri, is a poignant image immortalized in the records of the Indian Air Force. Mrs Sekhon later remarried.

Freelance researcher Air Cmde (Retd) Ramesh V Phadke, who was Nirmal Jit Singh Sekhon's course mate, has helped recreate the atmosphere of the Srinagar airfield by sharing his memories and research for the under-publication book, Air Power and National Security.

Arun Khetarpal

Battle Of Basantar, Shakargarh Sector
16 December 1971

Seated inside the cramped Famagusta, his Centurion battle tank named after a port in Cyprus, 2ⁿᵈ Lieutenant Arun Khetarpal is watching with narrowed eyes the enemy tanks before him. Most of them are wrecked and burning, the flames filling the sky with billowing grey smoke. He is trying to judge the trajectory of the shot his gunner has just fired. He will know if it has hit home because the moment a tank is hit the Pakistanis raise their gun and run out. Their religion forbids them a death by burning.

A vein is throbbing madly in Khetarpal's neck. If he manages to get this one, his tally will be five. He knows his tank is already on fire and exposed. He has switched off the radio set because he is being asked to pull back. His gun is still firing and he wants to get the bastards. He knows changing his position will give the enemy an opening. He will not let that happen.

There is a deadly whistling sound as a shell shoots in through the cupola of Khetarpal's tank. In that split second, he doesn't realize it has ripped his stomach—he is surprised when the confined interior of the tank fills with the acrid stench of burning flesh. Then it moves further, smashing into his thigh. It shatters the bone and bends it at an angle that traps it under the seat of his tank.

Bleeding profusely, all he can whisper hoarsely to his gunner Sawar Nathu Singh, who is imploring him to climb out of the tank, is: 'I won't be able to do it.' With that, Khetarpal collapses, guts spilling out of the bloody wound in his abdomen. It is around 10.15 a.m. The date: 16 December 1971. Khetarpal, breathing his last, is 21.

October 2013

Shortly after a U-turn from Ghitorni metro station is a small Indian Oil petrol pump with a narrow path on the left marked 'Forest Lane'. Follow that and you come to a massive iron gate with a nameplate saying 'Khetarpals'. Inside is a beautiful old farmhouse, quietly getting soaked in Delhi's retreating monsoon shower. There I find one of the most celebrated Param Vir Chakra awardees 2nd Lt Arun Khetarpal's 87-year-old mother. Scampering around her is a young golden retriever wagging her tail and pushing her wet nose into my palm before settling down to chew on a rubber bone. The lady on the wheelchair has very short white hair, withered, old hands and tired eyes that look at me wearily. She is trying to piece together fading memories of the son she lost 42 years ago.

Neither Mrs Khetarpal nor I want to revisit today the bloody battlefield of Basantar from where Arun never returned one cold December day. We'd rather talk about what he was like as a little boy. Was he quiet or outspoken, gentle or boisterous? Did he plead to sleep with his parents when the lights were turned off in his bedroom? Did he catch tadpoles in stagnant pools of rainwater or did he chase butterflies in the garden? Did he part his hair on the right or left? Did he pull his shoes off without untying their laces?

I want to know these little things about the hero I don't know. About those times when he would faithfully follow the soldiers working in his Army officer father's house and listen wide-eyed to their war stories. When he would insist on eating in the langar with them and then come back and tell his father that one day he would join the Army too. I want to know about the times he would coax his grandfather, his head on the old man's lap and little fingers entwined in dry, calloused ones, to tell stories of the Partition.

Maheshwari Khetarpal wants to tell me all this. For close to an hour she tries. She lets his name roll lovingly on her tongue, she tries to put her thoughts together, to string them into coherent words. But all that she can come up with are long meandering sentences that don't say much. The truth is that memory has failed her. Eventually, she gives up. 'Arun hamara beta tha. Par ab hamein kuchh yaad nahin.' (Arun was our son. But I remember nothing now.) Her voice is tinged with helpless frustration. Behind her, his hands on his waist, is a black and white photograph of the young and good looking 2nd Lt Arun Khetarpal. He smiles at the two of us from his mother's bedroom wall.

I switch off my Dictaphone and begin to tell her about the son she cannot remember—the eight-year-old boy from St. Columba's School, Delhi, who carried his younger brother's schoolbag on his back, held his hand and walked two and a half miles home from Gole Dak Khana to Sangli Mess when the car didn't come to pick them up one afternoon. I tell her how brave he was, not letting his little brother sense his fear even for a moment, and bursting into tears only when he was safely home in his mother's arms. I tell her about that afternoon in Shillong when he came back from school without his cardigan. He had given it away to a poor child and lied that it was lost. He was six then. I tell her about the day he got his first salary and how he sent some of it to his grandfather with the message: 'Dadaji, please accept my humble offering.' I tell her about the time he returned from the Lawrence School, Sanawar, and was thrilled to be mistaken for an Army officer at a party since he was so confident and dignified. I tell her about the teenager who joined the National Defence Academy, excelled at swimming and played 'Auld Lang Syne' on his clarinet at parties in cosy sitting rooms and translate for her the Robert Burns poem; she listens as if for the first time.

Mostly the old lady with very white hair cut really short sits on her wheelchair and continues to sip the tea that has grown cold in her hand. She slowly scoops spoonfuls of namkeen into her mouth with shaky fingers. I steady the cup and saucer on her lap each time it tilts, fearing the tea will spill on to her cotton nightdress.

I have just one more question for her. Did she send her elder son, then only 21, to war with the words: 'Your grandfather was a brave soldier, so was your father. Fight like a lion and don't come back a coward.'?

She is using all her willpower to raise the cup to her lips without spilling the tea. She lets it stay in midair, and looks at me.

'Kya aapne aisa kaha tha?' (Did you say that?) I ask again.

'Haan, kaha tha,' Yes, I said that, she says, her voice strong. On her wrinkled face is a glimmer of pride.

Winter, 1971

The train whistle shrieked, there was a deep shudder, a jolt, and then the rush of people getting on in a hurry. The Punjab Mail had started to move out of New Delhi railway station. Arun was hanging from the door, waving. His brother Mukesh, studying at IIT, Delhi, was walking along with the moving train, looking at him with envy mingled with anxiety. Arun lifted his eyes to his parents, Brigadier and Mrs Khetarpal, standing on the platform and moving farther from him with every passing moment as the train picked up speed. His father's arm was around his mother, strained smiles on their faces. He knew they were all trying to be brave. He smiled back at them and then lifted his right hand in a crisp salute. By that time the train had moved too far for him to see the glint of tears in his mother's eyes.

Many young officers had been recalled from the Young Officers course they had been attending at Ahmednagar when the war with Pakistan broke out. Second Lieutenant Arun Khetarpal was one of them. He and his unit officer Second Lieutenant Brijendra Singh had got on to a train to Delhi without a reservation. There were no seats for them and they had wangled some space in the pantry car. At Delhi, when they had had a few hours to change trains, Arun had unloaded his motorcycle and ridden it to his parents' house in Naraina to leave it there. He had returned in time for the Punjab Mail, happily lugging his blue patrol uniform and golf clubs. When Singh asked him why he needed the clubs and the ceremonial uniform on his way to fighting a war, Arun grinned: 'I plan to play golf in Lahore. And I'm sure there will be a dinner night after we win the war so I'll need the blue patrol.'

Wars were not new to the Khetarpals. Arun came from a family of soldiers. His great-grandfather had been in the Sikh army and fought against the British. His grandfather had served in the British Army during World War I and Arun's father, Brig. M.L. Khetarpal, was a Sapper. After studying at Sanawar, Arun had decided to become an Army officer and had joined the National Defence Academy in 1967. He was commissioned into 17 Poona Horse, an armoured or tank unit of the Indian Army, on 13 June 1971. He had been in the Army six months when the war broke out.

---

15 December, 11 p.m.

The winter night is pitch-dark. The young wheat in the fields is rustling gently in the breeze. In the daytime it had shimmered a brilliant green. At night it is like a soft carpet that shows the tracks of the tanks that have passed over it like ghosts of the night, crushing the fresh fronds under their weight.

The massive Centurion tanks of the Poona Horse are moving in a single file. Each is locating the one in front by the tiny glow of a red tail light small as the tip of a burning cigarette, directed at the ground so that it cannot be seen by enemy tanks or aircraft, only the tank following it. Their instructions are clear. They have to cross a 1500 square yard minefield strewn with anti-tank and anti-personnel mines to reach the infantry in the bridgehead. They have to do it fast.

That same morning, the commanding officer of 16 Madras had reported that enemy tanks were gathering for a major counterattack and unless the Indian tanks reached them quickly they would not be able to hold on much longer. The retreating Pakistani army had left behind anti- tank and anti-personnel mines. It was up to the engineers to breach this minefield and make a safe passage for the tanks. As the engineers were clearing the minefield with the trawls, the tanks of the regiment started moving behind them so they could speed up the induction into the bridgehead.

When Colonel (retired) S.S. Cheema, Sena Medal, talks about the war he says every single action flashes in front of his eyes as if it happened yesterday. He was a company commander with 3 Grenadiers and had played a key role in the daring attack on Jarpal as well as holding on in the bridgehead against the subsequent counter attacks by the enemy. It was a joint operation with 17 Horse, 4 Horse (the two armoured regiments) and 16 Madras. He recollects how Lieutenant Colonel Hanut Singh, the commanding officer of 17 Horse, decided that as the trawling by the sappers was going on to clear the minefield, his tanks would follow simultaneously, so that they could save precious time. He knew how much enemy pressure was building against the infantry in the bridgehead and realized that the tanks had to get there fast if they wanted to win this war. 'It was the most super-coordinated effort by the regiment and the engineers,' says Col Cheema. 'The operation is still believed to be miraculous in military history since not one tank was blown up by a mine.'

16 December

The squadron commander of B Squadron, 17 Horse, asks for reinforcements as Pakistan's tanks have started counterattacking at Jarpal, in the Shakargarh Sector. This is the same area that has earlier been captured by 3 Grenadiers in an operation where Major Hoshiar Singh has got his PVC and Maj Cheema his Sena Medal. Captain Malhotra, Lt Ahlawat and 2nd Lt Khetarpal are sent to assist B Squadron. Such is the intensity of the battle that within minutes they have knocked off seven enemy tanks. However, Ahlawat's tank is hit and it is in flames. Just then Khetarpal's tank is also hit. Capt. Malhotra orders him to pull back and bail out. But Khetarpal is unstoppable. He starts to chase the withdrawing enemy tanks and even manages to shoot and destroy one. The enemy sends in more tanks.

In the course of this battle Khetarpal is severely wounded. He is asked to abandon his tank but he realizes that the enemy

*is continuing to advance in his sector and if he abandons his
tank they would break through. 'No Sir, I will not abandon
my tank. My gun is still working and I will get these bastards,'
is what he famously says on radio on being asked to fall back.
Malhotra tells him one more time: 'Don't be silly. You get out of
the tank, otherwise you and your crew will be killed.' Khetarpal
does not come on the air again. He has deliberately switched off
his set. Malhotra's gun has also stopped functioning which makes
Khetarpal feel even more responsible for stopping the attack.*

*Four enemy tanks are still advancing when he calmly sets about
shooting them one by one. The last tank that he shoots is barely
75 yards from him. This is the enemy squadron commander's
tank. ('It was really one against the other,' says Cheema, who
was holding the area west of Jarpal and was a witness to this
action.) Khetarpal shoots the enemy tank and the enemy tank
shoots him back.*

*Arun Khetarpal is dead, but he has by his intrepid valour
saved the day. The enemy cannot get the passage that it is so
desperately seeking. Not one enemy tank gets past Khetarpal.
Second Lieutenant Arun Khetarpal is awarded the Param Vir
Chakra for displaying the highest qualities of valour, leadership
and strength of purpose. The young man of 21 years has performed
an act of courage and self-sacrifice that goes far beyond the call
of duty.*

Brig. Khetarpal was shaving when the bell rang. He paused
for a second and heard his wife's footsteps going towards the
door. Mukesh was getting ready to go to college. All these days

they had been living in constant fear, ears glued to the radio, listening to war bulletins and analysing where the action was taking place. They knew a fierce tank fight had taken place in Basantar on 16 December. The brigadier had barely been able to eat any dinner that night. He knew that was the area where Arun's regiment would be deployed. But all that had passed, the war was over and the Khetarpals were waiting for Arun to return. They had even had Arun's motorcycle serviced and his room cleaned.

The front door opened. There was some conversation and then a sound that made his hand stop shaving and his blood freeze; the dry rustle of an envelope changing hands. He sensed the scream before he heard it. He ran across to the front door. A postman was standing there; his wife lying on the floor. In her limp hand was a telegram that said: 'Deeply regret to inform your son IC 25067 Second Lieut Khetarpal reportedly killed in action sixteenth December. Please accept sincere condolences.'

———

In Husainpur village of Nagaur district, Rajasthan, retired Risaldar Major Honorary Captain Nathu Singh still wakes up in the dark sometimes. These are the nights when his memories seep into his dreams.

He is 24 once again, a sawar in the Poona Horse, on the battlefield of Bara Pind, 40 km into Pakistan. Crouched inside the cramped interiors of Famagusta, his Centurion tank, he is watching the flames billow out of the destroyed tanks in front of him. The dead, the dying, the wounded are lost in the scream of shells and the drone of the air strike. Ten Pakistani tanks have been destroyed, of which Famagusta has smashed four. However, it has been hit too and is now on fire.

Tank driver Prayag Singh is pleading with 2nd Lt Arun Khetarpal: 'Saab, let's move back and douse the flames.' Khetarpal's face is as dark as the grey smoke emerging from the carcasses of Pakistani Pattons burning furiously on the battlefield. 'No!' he says, his voice cold and firm. 'Didn't you hear CO saab on the wireless? He said no one will pull back an inch.'

In his blue dungarees, Nathu Singh takes position as the gunner once again. In front of him the air is dark with fumes. Mingled with the heat from the flaming tanks is the stench of burning flesh. Right behind him stands his tall and handsome young commander, dark stubble covering his weary face. He is shouting: 'On tank.' Nathu Singh aims his gun and fires. The Pakistani Patton tank he has targeted fires back. The massive Centurion shudders and behind him he hears a blood-curdling scream. The shell has come in through the cupola. There is smoke and flesh all around. The loader's head has been ripped off.

The brave young Khetarpal has collapsed. His left leg is arched at an impossible angle. Nathu looks down to feel a wet patch and finds blood all over his hand. Splinters have cut deep into his legs.

He wakes up with a start.

———

Seventy-year-old Nathu Singh takes a noisy sip of his tea and smiles. Most days he wears a dhoti and kurta. Sometimes he goes around the village in his jeep. He hasn't been inside a tank for decades. His days in uniform are long gone. He has put on weight and moves with a shuffling gait. More than 40 years have passed but he still has nightmares about the Battle of Basantar. These nights he wakes up bathed in cold sweat and then lies back on his pillow and stares into the darkness till dawn.

'Other people might have forgotten him but I still dream of Khetarpal saab. I see tanks burning around me. Saab is telling me to fire. He is standing behind me with a half smile on his lips. "On tank, Nathu. Fire!" he is saying. And then I fire. Bahut bahadur aadmi the saab,' he says putting his ribbed glass of milky tea down on the floor, 'Other people might have forgotten him but he will keep coming in my dreams till I live. For me he will never die.'

This story is largely based on interviews with Mr Mukesh Khetarpal, Arun's brother; and Risaldar Major (Retd) Nathu Singh. Mrs Maheshwari Khetarpal died shortly after this piece was written.

Hoshiar Singh

Basantar Nala, Shakargarh Sector, Pakistan
15–16 December 1971

It is a chilly winter night. Across the shadowy sugar cane and wheat fields that the soldiers of 3 Grenadiers have already crossed flows the Basantar Nala. The water is not in spate and has taken on a gentle, white glow in the moonlight. Looking at its sublime stillness, one cannot guess just how frigid it is. Only after one dips the foot in and the wetness seeps into leather boots and socks, pricking the soles like hundreds of sharp needles does one realize it.

The 120-plus men of Charlie Company (led by Major Hoshiar Singh) and the 120 of Bravo Company (led by Major S.S. Cheema) wading across the river are oblivious to its beauty and, to an extent, even the coldness. What concerns them more is the near-constant shelling right in their face and the minefields that they know the Pakistanis have laid out on the other side, which they will have to cross to reach their objective—the village of Jarpal. The orders for the two companies are to attack around midnight and capture Jarpal from east and west.

In their parkas, helmets and ankle boots, with small packs on their back, the soldiers splash across the freezing nala in silence. Each time the ice-cold water lashes the skin it feels like a knife cutting into flesh. After a while their exposed bodies go numb and the men trudge on, water up to their knees, weapons held above their heads to protect them from getting wet. They carry 7.62 mm rifles and Sten guns while the radio operators have their pistols. Each of them has at least two grenades, if not more. These will be required in the close combat that is expected to follow. Their faces are smeared with mud and gunpowder from the shelling they have endured.

A grim-faced Maj Hoshiar Singh is standing by as his men go across one by one—trousers soaking wet, his Sten gun in his arms and head covered by a balaclava. He is known for not wearing helmets. The map of Jarpal stamped on his mind, he knows he has to attack in the dark; the enemy has to be taken unawares.

It is going to be a long night. What he does not know is that his company will be fighting one of the fiercest battles ever fought by the Indian Army, not just in terms of attack but also for the number of vicious counterattacks that come from the enemy.

Colonel (retd) Cheema, Sena Medal, who later commanded 3 Grenadiers, now lives in Jalandhar. He is preparing for a lecture on the '71 War to Army units. He has his maps, notes and slides ready and is brushing up his memory.

He and Maj Hoshiar Singh were young company commanders together in 1971 and he remembers with a chuckle how both were so eager to face action that fateful day when their commanding officer Col V.P. Airy was to announce which companies would attack the Jarpal area. 'Hoshiar and I were sitting next to each other,' he says. 'He turned to me and said he was going to be really upset if his company was not included in the attack. I told him if my company was not picked up I would go and have it out with the CO!'

When the announcement finally came, the two officers looked at each other and smiled. Both the companies would be participating in phase one of the attack. Hoshiar Singh's C Company had been ordered to attack Jarpal from the east and Cheema's B Company was to attack from the west. Their wishes had come true. Now the time had come to prove their mettle.

The two officers had been good friends since the '65 war, when Hoshiar Singh was a lieutenant and Cheema the battalion adjutant. The task given to their battalion then was to attack a village in the Bikaner sector and evict the enemy holed up there. Lt Hoshiar Singh was sent out for a reconnaissance mission where, on his own initiative, he went dressed as a local riding a camel. He mingled with the Pakistanis and boldly went behind enemy lines, coming back with crucial information about their placement and location. Based on this adventurous outing on 5 October 1965, he briefed the CO in great detail, disclosing the exact enemy position, for which he got a mention in the dispatches.

Hoshiar Singh had earned a good name for himself in 1965, but his true calibre would show up in the action in 1971.

———

The capture of Jarpal

After the men of 3 Grenadiers had crossed the international border, their first objective was the capture of Bhaironath temple, a Hindu temple where the enemy had positioned a platoon-strength of soldiers and three Sherman tanks.

By the time the Indian forces reached the village, it had been deserted by all civilians, who fearing an attack had fled. Shortly after the attack, the Pakistani soldiers fled too, leaving their tanks behind, which were captured by the Indian Army. The battalion then marched on to Bhagor Khurd and then across the first minefield to reach Fatehpur and Dinga Narain Pur. It was decided they would cross the Basantar Nala to establish a bridgehead. The plan was that 16 Madras would capture Saraj Chak in phase one while Jarpal and Lohal would be captured by 3 Grenadiers in phase two of the brigade attack.

The night the men of Cheema's B Company and Hoshiar Singh's C Company were wading across the freezing Basantar Nala was D-day. They had been given the task of capturing Jarpal from west and east by 12.30 a.m. on 16 December. It was a Herculean task. Not only was the area around Jarpal village heavily mined, it was also occupied by a company of the enemy, which sat there with its deadly machine guns ready for action.

The moment the attacking companies crossed the nala,

emerging with soaked clothes, they encountered a minefield of about 1500 yards. Though the mines were embedded in the soil, they were easy to identify since the Pakistanis had wired the mined area on both sides to warn their own tanks and soldiers and to keep cattle out. Luckily for the infantry, most of these were anti-tank mines which wouldn't explode under a man's weight and the soldiers could cross these patches at night. The forming-up place or FUP where the men had to assemble and then proceed on their company missions was 1500 yards from Jarpal. It was very difficult to identify the objective at night because of the dark and enemy fire. 'We were told by the CO, "naak ki seedh mein chalte raho (keep walking straight),"' remembers Col Cheema. And that was exactly what the soldiers did, supported by their own artillery and mortar attack, which was aimed at keeping the enemy down.

Col (retd) S.S. Punia was the mortar platoon commander during the operation. He now lives in Gurgaon and, when the battalion celebrates Jarpal Day, sits down to have a drink with his old colleagues who fought the war with him. He remembers how he was asked to deploy his mortars after the minefield was cleared. 'Our mortars could fire up to 6 km and we used them to neutralize the enemy that night while the B and C Companies attacked Jarpal. It was a fierce fight,' he remembers. 'We fired a record number of 800 bombs that night and during the counterattacks. The Pakistanis were chased away and those who were hiding in bunkers were made prisoners of war.'

Around 12.30 a.m. on 16 December, the company commanders sent the signal to their CO saying that east and west of Jarpal had been captured. The men then dug trenches and settled down to defend what they had won. Reports had already started coming in that the enemy would go in for a massive offensive to take back its territory. Maj Hoshiar Singh and Maj Cheema both knew that the toughest part of their task was yet to begin.

16–17 December

The Pakistanis launch a record number of six counterattacks to reoccupy Jarpal, but all of these are beaten back by the men of B and C Companies. The enemy soldiers start coming in wave after wave, starting at 3.30 a.m. on 16 December; the moment one lot is beaten back, another appears. Though each attack is neutralized by the men, the fatigue of fighting almost constantly with little or no time to rest and recoup is getting to them.

This is where Maj Hoshiar Singh and Maj Cheema stand by their side and egg them on with their words and action. Between attacks they eat the field rations they are carrying and drink tea that is quickly prepared in the trenches and sipped from their canteen caps, tiffin boxes and whatever else they can lay their hands on.

Then comes startling information from a listening post that Maj Hoshiar Singh has created near the Gazipur Reserve Forest, south of Jarpal, about 400 m away from where the soldiers have dug their trenches. The men radio Maj Hoshiar Singh, saying they have noticed activity in the forest and are certain the enemy is planning to attack from that side. Maj Hoshiar Singh tells them to stay very quiet and to not open fire as it would warn the enemy about their presence. Instead, he orders them to fall back and join up with the rest of the company.

Meanwhile, he informs his CO on the radio set of the coming massive enemy attack and he would need artillery support to beat it back. He also ensures that his men are on alert and have taken cover in the trenches they had dug during the daytime. The soldiers are strictly warned to keep silent with no movement, no coughing, no sneezing, etc. For hours, they wait in complete silence, their hands clasped firmly around their rifles, faces dark with fatigue.

Around 4 a.m. the final attack comes as expected. The Pakistani army has attacked Jarpal with two companies of 35 Frontier Force Rifles that are led by Col Mohammad Akram Raja, the CO. Maj Hoshiar Singh allows the enemy soldiers to get closer even as his men watch impatiently, rifles cocked. He orders them to not open fire till he says so. It is only when the enemy soldiers are in the range of 100–50 yards that he yells out: 'Fire.'

All hell breaks loose as his men give it all they have got— medium machine guns (MMGs), light machine guns (LMGs), rifles, mortar, the artillery starts firing at the advancing enemy soldiers, who are taken completely unawares. It is a bloody sight with the men screaming in pain as bullets and shells whip into their bodies. Each man, from either side, gives it all he has. Amidst war cries, exploding shells, mortar bursts, bullets and exchange of abuse, the fight continues well into the morning.

Maj Hoshiar Singh is hit by splinters from an artillery shell and his leg is badly injured. He refuses to be evacuated, despite being told to by his CO. Supported by a soldier, he continues to move from one trench to another, encouraging his tired men to not give up, inspiring them to hold on to their strength and courage.

When an MMG gun jams, he climbs into the trench and, fixing it himself, he uses it to keep up the firing.

The firing is called off only after all enemy activity has ceased. As many as 42 Pakistani soldiers are taken POW. When a final count is done in the daylight, 89 of the enemy are lying dead in front of the C Company trenches. Col Cheema remembers how Captain Bhatt, the adjutant of Pakistan's 35 FF, had told him: 'There are 350 lying dead and wounded with us, and now we will have to re-raise 35 FF.'

Amongst the dead are five officers, including Col Raja, who was leading the attack. He has been hit by an MMG burst right in the face and has died a hero's death. His arms are frozen in the position in which he had been holding his Sten gun. Col V.P. Airy later writes a tribute for Col Raja on the basis of which he is given Pakistan's second highest award for gallantry—the Hilal-e-Jurat.

Maj Hoshiar Singh has displayed personal bravery and dauntless courage, with complete disregard for personal safety in the face of heavy odds, for which he is awarded the Param Vir Chakra. He is one of the rare few to have won the medal alive.

Col Hoshiar Singh was born on 5 May 1936 in a small village called Sisana in Haryana's Sonipat district. He studied in a local school, later attending the Jat Higher Secondary School. He was a good student and an outstanding sportsman; an excellent volleyball player, he represented Punjab in the nationals. A senior officer of the Jat Regimental Centre noticed his excellent game at a match and implored him to join the

Jat Regiment, which he did. He was enrolled into 2 Jat and later commissioned into 3 Grenadiers. Those who knew him remember him as a simple, down-to-earth man who was very fond of eating halwa-choorma but when it came to war tactics, he was said to have the cunning of a fox. After the capture of Jarpal when asked to indicate the location of his company, he did not do it from where the company was stationed. Instead, he moved 200 metres towards the enemy before firing the 2-inch illuminating mortar so that the enemy, if it was watching, would get confused. He conveyed the coordinates to his own CO on the radio set. He was a ground soldier and his field craft and understanding of enemy behaviour was one of the major reasons for the success in Jarpal. It was said that he could read the enemy's mind like a book.

Brigadier (retd) Randhir, who served with Hoshiar after the war says that while Hoshiar was a natural leader, he was also much loved by his battalion and a big favourite with his jawans and JCOs. He would always be by their side, constantly monitoring and supervising what they were doing. He also did not like punishing his men; he preferred to correct them with genuine affection. He knew his troops very well and could tell exactly how each man would behave in a particular situation. He went on to become a full colonel and died of a heart attack on 6 December 1998. Of his three sons, two are serving in the Army, and his wife, Dhanno, lives in Delhi with her son's family.

Brig. Randhir remembers the first time he went to join the battalion in early 1972 as a young officer. A ceasefire was in place, hostilities had ceased and though Jarpal was still to recover from the deadly shelling it had faced, sugar cane and wheat were growing in the fields, he says. Maj Hoshiar Singh and Maj Cheema were still holding fort at Jarpal after having chased the enemy right up to Barapind. He still remembers a prominent board that had been put up by the 54th Division just beyond the international border. It was a tribute to the big fight put up by the division, specially 3 Grenadiers, in capturing strategically important territory in Pakistan. It said: 'You are now entering Pakistan. No passports required. Bash on regardless.'

SIACHEN—1971

Siachen glacier, named after the pink sia blossoms that bloom across Ladakh in the summer months, has been called the battlefield on the roof of the world. Though no roses bloom in Siachen its beauty is not diminished for want of them.

Difficult to live in and visually striking, Siachen is home to some of the world's tallest mountains, their snow-capped tops giving way to rivers of white that gleam in the sun as they fall over coloured rocks. It is a mesmerizing landscape of towering peaks, ridges, deep crevices and velvet folds, with ice walls that rise a mile high and hug the clouds.

For a soldier, however, Siachen is the place where hell freezes over. It has been more than 28 years since India and Pakistan have been at war at those 18,000-feet-plus altitudes, where temperatures drop below -40 degrees and winds blow at speeds above 45 km an hour.

Siachen, the second longest glacier in the world, is a 75-km-long river of slow-moving ice surrounded by stupendous towers of snow. Men live in helicopter-maintained posts, they walk for days to reach their locations and are often out of touch with family and friends and the rest of the world. They lead a life of inhuman isolation in the most inhospitable terrain. They breathe air so cold and so deficient in oxygen that sometimes body organs cease to function, bringing a painful death. Fainting spells, loss of appetite, memory loss, loneliness and unbearable headaches are frequent. Sweat freezes inside gloves and socks, just another way for frostbite to chew its way through digits and limbs.

The enemy is not only hard to spot in the crevices and craters in the vast whiteness, he is also hard to hit. Rifles must be thawed repeatedly over kerosene stoves, and machine guns need to be primed with boiling water. While some troops fall to hostile fire, far more perish from the cold, the avalanches and from falling into snow-covered crevasses. The weather, they say, is your worst enemy.

Siachen has been a bone of contention between India and Pakistan soon after Independence. In the Karachi Agreement of 1949, both countries drew the ceasefire line across maps of Jammu and Kashmir from Manawer in the south to Khor in the north and then north to the glaciers through NJ 9842. When they came up to the glaciated wilderness of snow and ice they stopped at grid point NJ 9842, presuming that neither side would be interested in an area where not a blade of grass grows and it is a challenge to even stay alive and breathe here.

Pakistan however complicated the issue by ceding 5180 square kilometres of Indian territory to China in the area where the boundaries of India, China and Pakistan meet. Then they started permitting and assisting foreign mountaineering and scientific expeditions to explore areas that did not belong to them. Concerned by Pakistan's activities and getting wind of Pakistan's plans to move into the area, the Indian Army in 1983 made a pre-emptive move and occupied the Saltoro Ridge area on the glacier. In 1987, a misadventure was initiated by Pakistan when it ordered its troops to set up a post in Indian territory. A crack team of the Special Service Group (SSG) launched a surreptitious raid to occupy a key peak in Indian territory which they succeeded in and subsequently named Quaid Post after Quaid-e-Azam Mohammad Ali Jinnah. Quaid Post was at 21,153 feet above sea level on a massive mass of ice known as Bila-Fondla.

This was a challenge that the Indian Army could not ignore. It became imperative to take the peak back, throw the Pakistanis out and this was where Sub Maj (Hony Captain) Bana Singh stepped in and earned for himself a Param Vir Chakra. The post was renamed Bana Post and it is a coveted assignment for battle-hungry young officers of the Indian Army.

Stephen P. Cohen, an authority on the Indian subcontinent at the American think tank Brookings Institution, has famously called the fight over Siachen, 'a struggle of two bald men over a comb'. According to a statement made by Lt Gen M.L. Chibber, who was Northern Army Commander at the time of occupation of Siachen, 'This bleeding ulcer has cost us nearly 20,000 casualties in over twenty years and an estimated daily expenditure of two crores. India's military occupation of Saltoro Passes in spring 1948 was meant only to deter the Pakistanis from getting there first. The Indian Army had no plans for permanent occupation. At the end of the day, the Siachen conflict was a mistake.'

'Siachen is an awful place where you can step on a thin layer of snow and, poof, down you go 200 feet,' Gen Khalid Mehmood Arif, retired former vice chief of Pakistan's military, has said. 'But no nation ever wants to lose a single inch of territory, so Siachen has psychological and political importance. Its value is in ego and prestige.'

There have been talks of making Siachen a peace park but many defence analysts feel that in matters of national security, neither expenditure nor casualties matter.

References

Param Vir–Our Heroes in Battle by Maj Gen Ian Cardozo

The Coldest war; Frozen in Fury on the Roof of the World by Barry Bearak, published 23 May 1999, *The New York Times*

Indian Defence Review—Strategic Importance of Siachen by Maj Gen Sheru Thapliyal, Issue Vol. 21.1, Jan–Mar 2006

Bana Singh

In the tiny village of Kadyal near Jammu, in a small house surrounded by mustard fields, an old Sikh gets up at 4.30 every morning. He has a big glass of chai before heading to the neighbourhood gurudwara for ardaas (prayers), returning only at 8 a.m.

After a hearty breakfast of makke ki roti and sarson ka saag, he takes out his tractor and heads for the fields. It is the same routine through the year—the only thing that changes, with the seasons, is the crop: wheat in winter, sugar cane in summer, rice in the monsoon.

In January, however, retired Subedar Major (Honorary Captain) Bana Singh, Param Vir Chakra (PVC), opens his old black steel box and takes out his war medals to polish them till they sparkle. That is the time he goes to New Delhi to participate in the Republic Day Parade. Each time he holds the PVC in his hand, he remembers a very cold day in Siachen when the winds were blowing at 50 km an hour and sweat was freezing on his palms.

Saltoro Ridge, Siachen
25 June 1987

Small and slight, Naib Subedar Bana Singh of 8 J&K Light Infantry (8 JAK LI) was wading through waist-deep snow, his AK 47 rifle slung across his back. Above 19,000 feet, the days were no different from the nights and it was impossible to tell what time it was. A short while before, icy winds had been blowing at more than 40 km an hour, striking the soldiers like bullets on their open faces. No sooner had the winds dropped than a snowstorm had started. The visibility was down to near zero. An impregnable grey mist had dropped around Bana Singh and the two soldiers trudging wearily through the snow. The temperature had dropped to −45 degrees, making the sweat on their palms and the breath from their nostrils freeze into needle-like icicles.

For a moment, Bana Singh wondered if the task before him was even possible. But he shook his head and refused to even consider it impossible. Instead he concentrated on placing one weary foot after another.

Maybe it was best that they couldn't see what was around, he thought. He was still to recover from the shock of seeing the bodies of his comrades, massacred in cold blood by the Pakistanis. Preserved by the extreme weather, they had been lying half buried under freshly fallen snow, their faces grotesque masks of ice, their weapons fallen beside their bullet-riddled bodies. Though he had told his eyes not to look, they had ignored his command and continued to scan the faces of the dead soldiers scattered like rag dolls. He instinctively knew they had found what he didn't want to look at. The crumpled body on the far side bore the handsome face of Second Lieutenant Rajiv Pande, his eyes blank and staring into nothingness.

Bana Singh froze. Only a few days back, the young and gutsy officer had been joking and laughing in the warm langar at Sonam Post. Now he was cold and dead. Bana Singh gritted his teeth and moved on.

Up ahead was the hazy outline of Quaid Post, at 21,153 feet, where the enemy soldiers were holed up. His task was to capture the post. 'I don't care if we lose every man. We want that post. They killed our men. We can't let that go unavenged. Unit ki izzat ka sawaal hai (It is a matter of the unit's pride),' the cutting words of his commanding officer echoed in his ears.

Bana Singh gestured to his companions to stop. Their orders were to wait for three other soldiers being sent as reinforcement. Using their ice picks, the men cut into the snow wall and made place to sit huddled together, drawing heat from each other's tired bodies. There they waited for the others to join them. Frozen, tired and hungry, they had to fight a war, when such a war had never been fought at those precarious heights ever before, anywhere in the world!

Saltoro Ridge, where Bana Singh and his men were operating, is close to the Everest in terms of climate and terrain. Not only were they above 19,000 feet where the oxygen deficit made even walking a challenge, the temperature would fall below −45 degrees Celsius and just survival would become a challenge. Now they had to fight the enemy and recapture the post. What made it more challenging was that the enemy was sitting at a height and could fire down at them anytime. However, the task had to be done because the Pakistanis had not only occupied the post by stealth but they were also firing at helicopters and had fired at and killed unsuspecting men from the 8 JAK LI patrol that had gone there earlier.

Second Lieutenant Rajiv Pande, Nb Sub Hemraj and 10 jawans were in the first patrol that was sent on a reconnaissance of the area. The team was specially trained in skiing and mountain warfare, yet it was a Herculean task for them to fix ropes and scale the ice in that thin air. Every step was a challenge, but they persevered for over 48 hours in the sub-zero temperatures. When the post was just 500 m away, Pande asked his commanding officer Colonel A.P. Rai for further orders on the radio set. He was told to advance. The patrol did not realize that Pakistan's SSG commandos were watching them from an overhang, waiting for them to come within firing range. The moment the unsuspecting men came closer, the Pakistanis opened fire, killing all but two soldiers. Pande and his men died but the ropes they had tied would show Bana Singh and his team the way. Their dead faces would also fill the soldiers with sadness and cold fury, giving them the strength to go on.

The very next day, shocked by the cold-blooded killing of the men, senior officers of the Indian Army rushed to Sonam Post. These included the corps commander, the Army chief, and the defence minister. Col Rai, who had lost his men in the terrible shootout, was bristling with rage. He pleaded for another chance to take over the post. A full-fledged attack was planned. A small camp was established ahead of Sonam Post. Five Cheetah helicopters did 400 sorties, flying on minimum fuel to maximize load-bearing capacity, and the post was equipped with rations, pup tents, arms and ammunition.

A team of two officers, three JCOs and 57 men was earmarked for the task. Nb Sub Bana Singh did not figure in the selected team but Col Rai handpicked him for the task. 'Bana will go,' he said, 'I have a lot of faith in him.' No one knew at that time just how prophetic this inclusion was going to be. When Bana Singh was told he was going, he unquestioningly packed his rucksack, laced up his snow shoes and joined the others. Operation Rajiv had been launched to avenge the loss of 2nd Lt Pande and his team.

On 22 June, the first attempt was made to reach Quaid Post. During the night two jawans died of hypothermia, a dangerous condition where the organs start to shut down because of an extreme drop in body temperature.

It was decided that the next attempt would be made directly from Sonam Post. On 23 June, the men started climbing again at 8 p.m., but the high wind-velocity, deadly gaping crevasses and snowfall made it impossible to move ahead. The men also found it increasingly difficult to breathe in the rarefied air. By 4 a.m. they had only covered 150 metres.

They had to return to the camp disheartened, where they were met by a furious Col Rai, who had arrived by helicopter. 'Hamari joota parade hui,' Sub Maj Bana Singh now recollects with an embarrassed smile. 'Aur honi bhi thi. Hamara kaam tha, hame karna tha.' (We were summoned for a dressing-down. And it was right too. It was our job. We had to do it.) Col Rai told the men in no uncertain terms that he wanted the post. 'The post has to be captured. We cannot let the deaths of Rajiv and his men go unavenged,' he thundered as the men listened silently.

The very next day (24 June), the ropes were tied once again, this time in the same direction that Pande's ill-fated patrol had taken. At 8 p.m., the climb began once again. The task force commander Maj Virender Singh was the first to go, saying he would not hesitate to shoot anybody who turned back. 'The mission will be completed this time,' he said, his voice colder than the wind. With that he turned and pulled himself up by the rope dangling in the snow. The men followed.

They reached the exact spot where the earlier patrol had been massacred. The bodies of their comrades lay buried in the snow around them. All discomforts were forgotten in the rush of adrenaline and the desire to seek vengeance. Right above the men was the critically positioned overhang from where the Pakistanis had shot the entire team. Luckily the snowstorm and cold winds that had reduced visibility drastically also made the enemy complacent in their confidence that the Indians would never think of an attack in such bad weather conditions. The terrible pall of grey around them was deadly for the climbing soldiers, since it hid the gaping mouths of treacherous crevasses. Two of the men slipped and fell to their deaths. Some were injured and had to be left behind. Some fell, but climbed back to rejoin the attack team. But no one waited for anyone this time. They just kept moving ahead. One by one, more soldiers were lost or evacuated because of injuries, chest trouble and frostbite.

Finally, only Bana Singh and two others managed to reach Quaid Post. About 15 m away from it, they sat huddled together in the shelter they had cut in the snow and waited for the other soldiers so that they could attack the next day.

Quaid Post, 26 June

Bana and his comrades had spent the night in the snow. They had hardly been able to sleep in the extreme cold. Soon they saw three hazy figures walking in their direction. In their white snow suits and shoes, they looked like ghosts. Bana's blood froze and he reached for his rifle, but then he realized that the reinforcements had reached them. All five waited in the snow for a while and it was decided that they would attack the enemy post by 4.30 pm. They closed their eyes in prayer, and then Bana told them to start moving. The heavy, persistent snowfall did not abate and they trudged on, keeping a sharp watch for craters that had been covered by falling snow and meant a painful death.

Nb Sub Bana Singh led his men alone along the extremely dangerous route, climbing in near darkness. He inspired them with his indomitable courage and leadership. Despite the bad weather and the screaming winds the six brave men reached the post and stormed it. Flinging grenades into the enemy bunker, the men charged at the enemy soldiers. Bana Singh reached for a grenade and flung it inside a bunker, latching the door from outside. He didn't let the screams of the dying men distract him and charged with all his might, bayoneting those who were outside, taking them completely by surprise. Some ran down the slope into the Pakistani side, some were killed, others injured. Maj Virender Singh and two more soldiers had also joined Bana by then. With their light machine gun on single-shot mode since the guns had stopped firing more than once at a time in the extreme cold, Bana directed the fire at enemy soldiers who were trying to climb back. The soldiers were either killed or scared away. However, realizing that their post had been captured, they started shelling it.

Maj Virender received four bullets in his chest and stomach but refused to be evacuated. He told Bana Singh to try and capture the enemy alive, to which Singh shook his head and famously replied: 'Sir, these bastards are not my cousins!' It made the injured officer smile even in those moments when they were courting death. Rifleman Om Raj's arm was blown off by a shell and hung loosely by his side as he gasped in shock and pain. Bana Singh tried to stem the bleeding with bandages from his first-aid kit, but he couldn't. Both Om Raj, who was losing blood fast, and Maj Virender were taken a little lower down, where the weather had opened up and a helicopter could land to evacuate them. While Maj Virender survived and later rose to the rank of Brigadier, Om Raj died on the glacier in the arms of the men he had climbed up with. Both the men received Vir Chakras for their bravery.

On 27 June 1987, Brigade Commander Brigadier C.S. Nugyal climbed up to the post. In a rare, emotional moment he hugged fiercely the dirty and war-ravaged Bana Singh and his men. The post would thereafter be called Bana Top, he declared. Nb Sub Bana Singh was awarded the PVC for conspicuous bravery and leadership under the most adverse conditions. Operation Rajiv also resulted in the award of one Maha Vir Chakra, seven Vir Chakras and one Sena Medal, besides the PVC. The CO and the commander were awarded Uttam Yudh Seva Medals.

Sixty-five now, Sub Maj Bana Singh, PVC, who was born in Ranbir Singh Pora tehsil of Jammu and Kashmir on 6

January 1949 in a Sikh family, sits in his small house, amid emerald-like green wheat fields. He finishes his story with a sigh. 'I was 19 when I joined the Jammu & Kashmir Light Infantry. I wouldn't say what I did in Siachen was an act of bravery. I just fulfilled my responsibilities as a soldier. We succeeded. Had we not succeeded I would not be sitting here before you alive,' he says.

———

Srinagar, 16 March 2008

A dark, slightly portly Sikh gentlemen in a light-coloured suit and turban watches keenly as the marching contingent of the passing-out parade stomps across the Bana Singh Parade Ground of the JAK LI Regimental Centre at Rangreth. He smiles when the Bana Singh Medal is announced for the recruit with the best drill and a slim, young, sprightly boy marches up smartly to collect it. Among the young soldiers is Rajinder Singh, who his father Bana Singh has come to watch. Two decades after Bana performed an act of unmatched heroism on the freezing heights of Siachen, his 18-year-old son joined 8 JAK LI, the regiment Bana began his career in.

Parade over, the proud father smiles to himself and gets up to join the other parents for tea. He will return to his village and a retired life. A baton has been passed on.

This story is based on conversations with Sub Maj (Retd) Bana Singh

OPERATION PAWAN
1987−90

The strained relations between the Sinhalese, in a majority in Sri Lanka, and the Tamils, who constitute less than 20 per cent of the population, was the reason for the Sri Lanka crisis.

In the 1970s, the Tamil United Liberation Force, a separatist Tamil nationalist group, started demanding a separate state of Tamil Eelam that would give the Tamilians more autonomy. When all peaceful initiatives failed they resorted to violence.

The movement found support with the Tamils in Tamil Nadu, who gave sanctuary to the rebels and supported them with financial aid, arms and ammunition. In 1986, the Sri Lankan government stepped up their action against the insurgency. In 1987, the Sri Lanka Army laid siege on the town of Jaffna, resulting in many civilians dying.

India feared a backlash from the Tamils living in south India and decided to intervene. On 29 July 1987, an agreement was signed between the Sri Lankan government and India in which Tamil leaders were also involved.

In keeping with this, an Indian Peace Keeping Force (IPKF) was inducted into Sri Lanka in August. The militants were to surrender their arms to this force, which was meant to be a peaceful procedure, in which elections would follow and Tamils would be given more autonomy. The IPKF's role was to ensure the return of peace. However, the move backfired. While other militant groups laid down their arms, the Liberation Tigers of Tamil Eelam (LTTE) surrendered very few weapons and some of them even committed suicide by swallowing the cyanide capsules they wore around their necks while they were in Sri Lankan custody.

The LTTE now unleashed a wave of violence against the IPKP who were left with no option but to retaliate. On 10 October 1987, the Indian force went into action in north Jaffna. They faced heavy losses due to lack of proper intelligence backup, unfamiliar terrain and guerilla attacks by the LTTE, which used children and women as soldiers, against whom the Indian Army found it very difficult to retaliate. Though initially only 54 Division had gone into action; soon three more divisions—4, 36 and 57—were inducted.

Without proper maps or guidance, troops had to fight at a disadvantage. They were also demoralized by the fact that the LTTE were being supported by Tamils in India.

A very difficult war was fought where many brave soldiers lost their lives. Maj Ramaswamy Parameswaran of 8 Mahar was decorated with the Param Vir Chakra posthumously for his valour and leadership and extreme devotion to duty under such trying circumstances.

Ramaswamy Parameswaran

North Jaffna
24 November 1987

The time is 7 p.m. Dusk has fallen over north Jaffna, Sri Lanka. The sky is dark with rain clouds when the men of Alpha Company, 8 Mahar, start marching towards Kantharodai, ready to fire the self-loading rifles in their hands. They are deployed at Uduvil Girls College, and are now out on patrol since information has come that a consignment of arms and ammunition is being unloaded at the house of the headman of Kantharodai village, a man called Dharmalingam. The patrol of 10 soldiers is being led by Captain D.R. Sharma, A Company's second-in-command.

Kantharodai is a small village that comprises a few huts surrounded by dense coconut groves. The soldiers walk as quietly as they can, finding their way in the darkness. The area around them is swampy and filled with coconut trees and deep undergrowth; there are no street lights and they have been told not to use any lights as they will draw attention to them. As they trudge along, Sharma has this nagging feeling that they are being watched by LTTE (Liberation Tigers of Tamil Eelam).

A few single-storied houses nestle among the clusters of trees. Sharma reports to his company commander Major Ramaswamy Parameswaran—or Parry sahab, as his troops affectionately call him—that they have been fired at by the LTTE militants from a temple and the militant strength appears to be much larger than anticipated. Parry has been posted to 8 Mahar for less than two months. He has been picked since he is a Tamilian and can speak the local language. Also officiating as the battalion quarter master after the battalion lost Capt. Sunil Chandra in an earlier operation, he is raring to come to the aid of his men. He has been functioning as quarter master during the day, looking after rations and stores, and taking on the mantle of A Company commander at night. He quickly puts together another patrol of 20 jawans and junior Commissioned Officer (JCO) Sampat Sable and joins up with the first patrol.

It is around midnight when the combined patrol of 30 soldiers starts moving towards Kantharodai. It has begun to rain and the soldiers cover the mouths of their guns with polythene sheets. Some of them have ponchos but since they are inconvenient to wear, most prefer to get wet in the slow-falling rain.

They keep walking in a column in the pitch dark, cautiously covering 4.5 km while making sure that the coconut groves and swamp around the road are free of LTTE. Around 1.30 a.m., the patrol reaches Dharmalingam's house. It is set in an acre-plus compound and has a pond, coconut trees and even a garden.

Everyone appears to be sleeping since the house is in darkness. The weather has worsened. The rain is now coming down in a thick downpour and the night sky is streaked with flashes of lightning and the sound of thunder. The men are soaking wet by now, water is seeping out of their heavy wood-soled DMS boots that have become bulky with moisture.

They surround the house and squat about 800 m from it in groups of 10. No movement is detected, but they see an old truck parked nearby, next to what appears to be a garage. This lends credibility to the reports of the weapon consignment being unloaded there. Not risking attacking in the dark, the men wait for dawn. They squat in the grass even as the rain falls and are told not to move, cough or get up even to relieve themselves.

Around 5.30 a.m., the family's dogs start barking and Parry decides to search the house. While the rest of the soldiers close in, he, Sharma and radio operator Dilip Maske go in and bring out Dharmalingam and his family. But even a thorough search yields nothing suspicious and it is decided that the patrol will return to headquarters. The officers shelter in a deserted house and discuss the route they should take to go back, deciding on the tarred Kantharodai–Uduvil road again since they want to avoid the waterlogged marshy terrain where LTTE ambushes are expected.

Unfortunately for them, the road goes past a pond with three temples around it, where LTTE militants have sought shelter. Later, much later, it is surmised that since Maratha Light Infantry were operating west of the 8 Mahar area, the LTTE cadre that Parry and his men run into may have accidentally drifted on to the path of this returning patrol. Now, however, the soldiers do not know all this or even that they have been *spotted by LTTE, who are watching them silently, waiting for a chance to attack.*

————

It is 6.30 a.m. when the tired, rain-soaked and sleep-deprived soldiers are passing the pond. A burst of heavy machine gunfire (HMG) hits Sepoy Jeevan Athawale. Sepoy Jagan Lal, who is behind him, shoots and kills one militant but is caught in a burst of light machine gunfire (LMG). At this moment, the militants open fire from all three temples, scattering the entire patrol.

'We were walking on the road, spread out over 300 meters. Sampat Sahab was leading with 10 jawans; he was followed by Capt. Sharma Sahab with 10 jawans and Parry Sahab was bringing up the rear with 10 jawans. Just then the HMG fire came and hit two of our men,' says Subedar (Retd.) Dilip Maske, who retired as a JCO and now works as assistant manager with a security firm in Aurangabad. The two soldiers responsible for the LMG are badly injured in the legs. They fall and their LMG drops on the road. The soldiers walking in front also get pinned down because the fire starts coming from all directions and suddenly the air is full of deadly flying bullets.

The soldiers drop to the ground and Parry orders them to take immediate cover in the forest on the other side of the road. Picking up the dropped LMG, the men crawl into the thick undergrowth, taking their injured comrades along. Both are bleeding profusely from the bone-shattering shots. The soldiers go about 5 m into the forest and take cover in a thicket of coconut trees. From there, they try to return the fire, but it is a futile exercise since the militants cannot be seen. Parry and Sharma decide that former will move *in from the east and the latter from the west and north.*

Capt. Sharma and Sepoy Jarnail Singh pick up their rocket launcher and walk into the pond since they need open space to use it. Standing in the water, they direct a few bursts at the temple from where the most fire is coming; they can't do much since the HMG fire keeps coming and have to return looking for cover. During this exercise, Jarnail is hit by an LMG burst on his left leg that cripples him, but he drags himself into an under-construction house. Sharma's team decides to take shelter there. There are two more houses in the area and the soldiers have unknowingly walked into an ambush. Naik Appanna Sarje comes out of the house to fire and almost walks into two militants. He kills one but the other manages to escape. As he tries to fire at the fleeing militant, he is shot and falls down, mortally wounded. Capt. Sharma asks Jarnail to fire a rocket at the house sheltering the LTTE militants, but the round misfires. The aerial of the radio set with them breaks and they are not able to make any transmissions either. Just then, they spot two militants looking in through the window, and before they can react, the militants lob a grenade inside. Sharma, who is trying to get through to the battalion HQ by hooking his set to a radio aerial in the house, miraculously gets through. He shouts at Jarnail to pick up the grenade and throw it out of the window, but even as the injured Jarnail bends to do so, the grenade bursts and the flying shards slash into him. Sharma escapes unhurt and starts lobbing grenades at the militants. Two of them fall and the soldiers watch from inside the house as their bodies are dragged away by their compatriots.

The soldiers face heavy firing from all directions. They have inadvertently walked into an LTTE hideout. The militants are holed up in spaces under the ceiling and even on top of the coconut trees. 'We did not know much about hideouts in those days and didn't realize that the rebels were hiding all around us. Capt. Sharma and Sampat Sahab, along with their columns, were caught in the ambush. There were immediate casualties,' remembers Maske. Radio operator Vidyasagar Dongre and Ramesh Athawale are injured in the fire; Rajan, who is trying to return the attack with mortar fire is hit by a burst that kills him on the spot. Ganesh Kohle, who is handling the LMG, is also shot dead. LTTE are using AK-47s, grenades, explosives and the deadly HMGs that inflict the maximum damage. They have even mined the area, which restricts the movement of the soldiers, who were completely at a disadvantage.

Parry sees the firing from his location and decides to step in to save the men. 'Sahab told us that our soldiers had walked into an ambush and we would go from behind and do a counter-ambush so that our men could be rescued,' recounts Maske.

Taking 10 men with him, Parry moves forward. Sepoy Raj Kumar Sharma and Naik Pandurang Dhoble are with him but the group breaks up under the intense fire coming at them. Parry does not lose his cool even for a moment. He fixes the LMG and tells Raj Kumar to fire at the militants. He decides that the rest shall move forward under cover of that fire. Raj Kumar has just started firing when an AK-47 burst from a treetop hits him, and he falls. The soldiers are pinned down by the incessant fire.

Parry refuses to be cowed down and, with absolutely no concern for his own safety, drops on his stomach and crawls forward through the coconut grove where many of the trees have been chopped down to about five feet. Taking cover behind a tree stump, Parry fires the LMG in the direction of the ambush. He startles the LTTE militants, who realize they have been surrounded.

Just then an HMG burst from a sniper, sitting atop of a coconut tree, catches Parry on his left wrist, smashing the bone to bits and nearly severing his hand. The impact is so high that it takes off his watch, which falls some distance away. Even as his men watch, Parry charges at the militant closest to him, completely disregarding his grievous injury. He snatches the man's weapon and shoots him, shouting at his men to follow.

Just then, another HMG burst hits him in the chest. In his pocket he has a Mini Clear pistol and rounds he has planned to use to send a success signal. They burst and the brave officer collapses, falling on his face. When his body is recovered by Capt. Sharma almost an hour later, his watch is found lying near him. It has stopped at 8.10 a.m. 'I was just three metres behind him,' says Maske. However, the fire is so intense that for a long time the soldiers are not able to even reach his body.

Though shocked by the loss of their brave commander, the six jawans are inspired by his sacrifice and continue to fight back. They can see the militants scattering in panic. 'They were young boys and girls in lungis (sarongs) and T-shirts. Most of them were carrying AK-47s though they did not have either helmets or slippers on their feet,' remembers Maske. The rebels start jumping out of their hideouts and running away while still firing at the soldiers.

The battalion has, meanwhile, sent reinforcements. Capt. T.C. Bhattacharya and 20 other ranks reach the location and start firing at the three temples. Bhattacharya enters the first temple and manages to catch a militant. It is a bold action that unnerves the other rebels and sends them fleeing. Bhattacharya succeeds in extracting information from his prisoner about a hideout from where three AK-47s, two rocket launchers, 200 booster charges and 100 kg of explosives are recovered. A team of 1 Maratha Light Infantry, led by Major Devendra Brar, also arrives. This party of 25 soldiers helps Maske and Ankush Waghmare move forward and retrieve Parry's body. It is brought to an empty house where Raj Kumar is given first aid. Slowly the firing stops.

Six militants are killed in the attack and an unknown number wounded. 8 Mahar loses Parry, Naik Appana Sarje, Rajan Lal and Milind Kohle, while nine others are wounded.

On 25 November, Parry's body is flown to Chennai and handed over to his kin. The three martyred soldiers are cremated with full military honours at Uduvil.

For his gallant act of bravery, exemplary leadership and command, Maj Ramaswamy Parameswaran is awarded posthumously the nation's highest gallantry award, the Param Vir Chakra. His saga of valour and selfless sacrifice will continue to inspire new generations of Mahar soldiers.

'The casualties would have been much higher had Parry Sahab not decided on going for a counter-ambush,' says Maske. 'He lost his life, but saved so many others.'

Parry, as Maj Parameswaran is affectionately remembered by his men, was a devoted and committed officer, who liked to lead by example. Jawans who served under him remember his considerate but firm command and quick forgiveness. He was an approachable man, who the soldiers could easily confide in. He would never humiliate a man by punishing him in public, but if someone was wrong, he would not let that go unchecked either. He is remembered by the men who were in the last patrol with him even today for saving their lives by putting his own on the line. He was a Tamilian fighting against Tamil militants, but he never looked at things that way. He considered himself an officer of the Indian Army first and was a perfect example of how soldiers rise above narrow constraints of caste and politics to become devoted citizens of a nation.

Parry was born on 13 September 1946 in Bombay to K.S. and Janaki Ramaswamy. He completed his schooling from SIES (South Indian Education Society) High School, Mumbai, in 1963 and his graduation in science from SIES College in 1968. In 1971, when India was fighting Pakistan, he joined the Officers' Training Academy in Chennai and passed out on 16 June 1972. He was commissioned into 15 Mahar and served there for eight years. In May 1981, he got married to Uma. In April 1983, he was sent to 5 Mahar.

Brigadier E.V. Reddy, a young lieutenant in 5 Mahar when Parry was a senior major with more than 10 years of service, remembers the couple posted at Dehradun, with a lot of affection. 'He was an affable, gentle guy, who could bring cheer into any gathering. She was a poet and writer and they were devoted to each other,' he says. The youngsters would often drop by at the Parameswarans' house for a meal and Brig. Reddy recounts how Parry would cook and feed them south Indian fare like idli and dosa. Parry was handpicked for 8 Mahar, which was the first unit of the Indian Army to land in Sri Lanka as part of the Indian Peace-Keeping Force, because he could speak Tamil. He was raring to go.

The peace-keeping operation had completely backfired and the Indian Army, which was initially tasked with ensuring peace and seeking surrender of Tamil militants, found itself fighting a hostile force. Since these were early days, the participating units did not have proper maps or intelligence and since the militants were freely using women and children, it was difficult for the men in uniform to retaliate against this civilian force.

It was while taking part in Operation Pawan as part of 91 Infantry Brigade, 54 Infantry Division, just a month and 20 days after he joined 8 Mahar, that Parry was destined to attain martyrdom in the battle of Kantharodai. Strangely enough, on 23 November 1987, Uma's mangalsutra broke at home in Dehradun where she had continued to stay after Parry left for Sri Lanka. She was really upset since she took it as a bad omen, but her friends told her not to be superstitious. Two days later, she received the news that her husband had lost his life fighting the Tamil rebels. She was completely shattered but has since remarried and picked up the pieces of her life.

NOTE

Capt. Sunil Chandra from 8 Mahar was commanding a squad when on 16 October 1987 he received news that another company located at Annaikottai had been surrounded and repeatedly attacked by the militants, causing heavy casualties. The soldiers needed an immediate replenishment of ammunition, which they had exhausted. An attempt was made to supply by helicopter, but that failed due to militants directing heavy fire at it. All routes to get there had also been blocked by the LTTE.

Capt. Chandra, along with 15 men, was detailed to take the reinforcements to the company. He left Uduvil at 7 p.m. on 16 October and fought his way through, despite being wounded in the leg. His party incurred eight casualties, and reached the besieged company on 17 October, when it had been left with just six rounds of 7.62 mm and two grenades. He was hit by an MMG burst in the chest, but crawled on till he reached the company and handed over the ammunition. Subsequently, he succumbed to his injuries. He was posthumously awarded the Vir Chakra.

The battle account was reconstructed from conversations with Subedar (Retd) Dilip Maske, who participated in the same operation

THE KARGIL WAR
1999

O f all the wars India fought none caught the imagination of the people as much as Kargil. This was the first war fought with constant media coverage. Indians until now obsessed with film stars got to see for the first time what real heroes looked like as television sets beamed right into our bedrooms images of armed soldiers and gritty young officers bravely climbing the peaks of Tiger Hill and Dras to flush out crafty intruders.

The Tricolor was eventually unfurled on every peak but many of these brave men never returned from the war. We were left with images of coffins being saluted and parents, spouses and little children weeping quietly at funerals that made every Indian realize the terrible loss that every conflict results in.

Attacks were launched at heights above 15,000 feet in sub-zero temperatures. Soldiers had to fight in an environment where even breathing is a strain. With heavy backpacks, they had to climb for days on meagre rations and sometimes nothing to eat and face bullet showers and grenade attacks to finally flush out the enemy sitting secure behind sanghars and bunkers and in snow tents.

The Indian government's decision to not let the Army cross the LOC reduced their tactical options greatly. Conditions were nightmarish for battalion commanders when uncompromising orders from the top demanded results almost overnight. These results were achieved but at a great loss. Twenty-five officers and 436 jawans were killed, and 54 officers and 629 jawans wounded at Kargil. Many were disabled for life.

It was in these daunting circumstances that four of the heroes of the Kargil War won their Param Vir Chakras. Two of these were officers and two jawans but only two could survive to tell their brave tales. About the other two we know from the accounts of comrades who fought besides them, witnessed their acts of glory and then brought their bodies home.

A backgrounder

The Pakistan offensive in Kargil was part of a much bigger plan by Pakistan and it took Indian policy planners by surprise. During the winter of 1998–99, some elements of the Pakistani Armed Forces were covertly training and sending Pakistani troops and paramilitary forces, some allegedly in the guise of mujahideen, into territory on the Indian side of the LOC. The infiltration was code named Operation Badr, and was aimed at severing the link between Kashmir and Ladakh and causing Indian forces to withdraw from the Siachen Glacier, thus forcing India to negotiate a settlement of the broader Kashmir dispute. Pakistan also believed that any tension in the region would help make the Kashmir issue international.

Pakistani Lieutenant General Shahid Aziz, then head of ISI analysis wing, later stated that there were only regular Pakistan Army soldiers who took part in the Kargil War. 'There were no mujahideen, only taped wireless messages, which fooled no one. Our soldiers were made to occupy barren ridges, with hand-held weapons and ammunition,' Lt Gen Aziz wrote in his article in the daily *The Nation* in January 2013.

By early May1999, Pakistan had extended its defences well across the Line of Control (LOC) in the Mushkoh, Dras, Kaksar and Batalik sectors. The extent of penetration across the LOC varied from 4 to 8 km in each sector. Strong defensive positions were established by regular troops of the Northern Light Infantry and Special Service Group commandos, with full support of artillery, mortar and anti-aircraft missiles. Military stores were dumped and anti-personnel mines laid. A force of 2000-strong had moved into Indian territory. They were directly overlooking the Srinagar–Leh highway.

The first reports that there were intruders came in from a bunch of shepherds on 6 May 1999 and it took the army time to determine the size and extent of the intrusion. A patrol that was sent out never returned and it was only on 10 June 1999 that the Pakistani Army returned to India the cruelly mutilated bodies of Maj Saurabh Kalia, the patrol leader, and his five soldiers. The bestiality of the Pakistani soldiers and the manner in which they had treated the Indian soldiers who had been taken prisoners was shocking. What was even worse was that the government of India, other than making a few statements, did not and has not till date taken the case up more strongly with the world bodies. Major Kalia's father is still waging a lone war against the war crime.

The extent of intrusion in Kargil, when it was fully known, was staggering. Fighting on mountains is always to the advantage of the defender who is secure behind his defences while the attacker who has been ordered to 'throw them out' is totally vulnerable in the open as he climbs steep slopes which are at times almost vertical and require the use of ropes. The defending Pakistani soldiers were very confident that the odds were so much in their favour that they could beat back any attack.

It would have been a difficult war to win but for one factor in the Indian armed forces that the enemy had not factored in—raw courage. Through sheer grit and determination, young officers in their 20s led their men to impending death, paving the way for others to follow.

Initially, without maps, supplies, adequate ammunition and even winter clothing, the ill-equipped infantryman fought and eventually won this battle for India. He was supported by the gunners who tried to reduce the odds by continuously bombarding the heights where the enemy soldiers were lodged and the Air Force pilots who fearlessly flew overhead and bombed the enemy bunkers.

In many vital points, neither artillery nor air power could dislodge the Pakistani soldiers, who were not in visible range. The Indian Army had no option but to send up soldiers for direct ground assaults which were slow and took a heavy toll, given the steep ascent that had to be made on peaks as high as 18,000 feet. Since any daylight attack would be suicidal, all the attacks had to be made under the cover of darkness, escalating the risk of freezing. Accounting for the wind-chill factor, the temperatures were often as low as –15 degrees Celsius near the mountaintops.

The high-risk frontal assaults could have been avoided if the Indian Arm had blocked the supply route of the enemy, virtually creating a siege, but this was not permitted since it meant Indian troops would have to cross the LOC, something that India was not willing to do since it would have reduced international support for its cause. The Army thus had to pay a very heavy price for diplomacy by losing brave young soldiers in circumstances that were biased against them.

According to India's then Army chief Ved Prakash Malik, and many other scholars, much of the background planning, including the construction of logistical supply routes, had been undertaken much earlier. Some analysts believe that the blueprint of attack, that had been sidelined by other political leaders, was reactivated soon after Pervez Musharraf was appointed chief of army staff in October 1998. After the war, Nawaz Sharif, prime minister of Pakistan during the Kargil conflict, claimed that he was unaware of the plans and that he first learned about the situation when he received an urgent phone call from Atal Bihari Vajpayee, his counterpart in India. Sharif attributed the plan to Musharraf and 'just two or three of his cronies', a view shared by some Pakistani writers who have stated that only four generals, including Musharraf, knew of the plan. Musharraf, however, asserted that Sharif had been briefed on the Kargil operation 15 days ahead of Vajpayee's journey to Lahore on 20 February.

Two months into the conflict, Indian troops had slowly retaken most of the ridges that were encroached by the infiltrators; according to official count, an estimated 80 per cent of the intruded area and nearly all high ground was back under Indian control.

Four brave soldiers were awarded the Param Vir Chakra for their supreme bravery in Kargil. They were:

1. Grenadier Yogender Singh Yadav, 18 Grenadiers, Param Vir Chakra.

2. Lieutenant Manoj Kumar Pandey, 1/11 Gorkha Rifles, Param Vir Chakra, posthumous.
3. Captain Vikram Batra, 13 JAK Rifles, Param Vir Chakra, posthumous.
4. Rifleman Sanjay Kumar, 13 JAK Rifles, Param Vir Chakra.

References

Param Vir—Our Heroes in Battle by Maj Gen Ian Cardozo
'The Kargil War 1999', *Bharat Rakshak*

Putting Our Children in the Line of Fire', by Gen Shahid Aziz, *The Nation*, 3 Feb 2014

'Nawaz Blames Musharraf for Kargil', *The Times of India*, 28 May 2006

Kargil Planned before Vajpayee's visit: Musharraf', *Indian Express*, 13 May 2006

Manoj Kumar Pandey

Batalik sector, Kargil
2–3 July 1999

Manoj Pandey sat crouched in a trench, almost blending in
with the rugged brown slope. He was watching a burst of
Bofors fire light up the purple sky. The unruly stubble on
his chin made his face itch. He could smell the nauseating
sweat in his hair even from under his helmet with a rip in the
lining where the hard metal pressed against his scalp—cold
yet strangely reassuring. Under the grime smearing his face,
his features were good—a well-defined straight nose, firm
mouth, broad forehead creased in concentration. He didn't
wear a moustache. His chin was determined, his eyes warm,
brown and finely lashed, though at that moment they were
bloodshot from serious lack of sleep. He sat motionless, staring

stonily ahead, his rough, weather-beaten hands clasped firmly around his Insas rifle.

A khukri (a traditional Nepali dagger) hung from his belt and rubbed against his thigh, the evil glint of its cunning blade sheathed in soft velvet. At the regimental centre in Lucknow, where he was trained to be a Gorkha Rifles soldier, he had been told it was the best weapon to use in close combat, small and deadly, instilling instant terror in the enemy. He had been trained to slice a man's neck off, cutting swiftly across the skin—right to left, left to right, ripping through veins and sinewy muscles in one powerful move. At the regiment's Dussehra celebration when he had just joined his unit two years ago, he had been asked to prove his mettle by cutting off the head of the sacrificial goat after the puja. For a moment his mind had wavered but then his arms had lifted in the air, bringing the glittering blade of the sharp dagger down on the scared, bleating animal's neck, severing it from its twitching body in one massive blow that sprayed his nervous, perspiring face with warm blood. Later, in his room, he had trembled at the act and washed his hands half a dozen times to take away the guilt of his first deliberate kill. He had always been a vegetarian and a teetotaller.

In the past two months, Manoj had come a long way from his natural humane reluctance to take lives. He had contrived attacks, planned kills and used stealth to surprise enemy soldiers as they sat on craggy peaks. He had climbed up freezing mountains, trudging through snow and sleet, even without winter clothing in the initial days. He would use woollen socks as gloves to shield his freezing fingers, peeling them off when they got soaked in a sudden shower, twisting them to squeeze the water out and slipping them on again. He had fixed targets within the sight of his rifle, taken aim and pressed the trigger; tracing the bullet's path with his eyes as it zipped through the distance and embedded itself in human flesh. He had killed in cold blood, shooting men through their heads, through their hearts, dispassionately watching them bleed to death.

His expertise with the khukri as a weapon of execution had, however, not been tested yet. His instinct told him that tonight could be the night.

Manoj Pandey shifted his weight and winced. The edges of his briefs were cutting into his groin. Every time he moved, the rough fabric would slice through the raw skin, digging a micro-inch deeper. He had been wearing the same clothes for almost a week.

Running a hand across his soiled combats, he felt the murky stiffness of sweat and grime. His fingers hovered over the rips and tears where the fabric had been ragged threadbare by crawling on razor-sharp rocks. But there was consolation in company. Cocking his head slightly, he silently observed the dark outlines of his men—short, stocky Gorkhas, grouped unevenly around him in the darkness—dirty, starving and battle-fatigued, yet brave. He made no sign, his eyes remained dark and languid, no emotion flitted across his face, but for them he felt deep warmth in his heart.

The sun had disappeared, dropping an impregnable black quilt over the terrain. It hid the crisp green of the grass, the blue rush of the sparkling water, the mesmerizing beauty of the district; and he preferred it that way. Daylight just added to his outrage at Pakistan's audacity to sneak in and occupy the heights around them. Emotion interfered with resolve; tonight all he needed was cold reason and an animal's instinct for survival.

Somewhere behind him, in the gloomy darkness intercepted only by the call of crickets, the Ganasak Nala gurgled, lapping against the quiet of the still night. Ahead loomed a steep though blurred 70-degree incline. That was Khalubar, the 5000-metre high ridge he and his men had to climb that night. Their task: to reach up undetected, take the enemy by surprise and destroy the Pakistani bunkers on top before daybreak.

He knew not many of them were expected to return but that didn't bother him much. He remembered the emotional words he had once scrawled in the depths of a diary he had been maintaining since childhood: Some goals are so worthy; it's glorious even to fail. Signalling to his men to follow with a curt nod, Manoj got up, slung his gun behind him and started to walk.

For more than a month they had been on almost continuous assignments, one following the other. In the Army, they called it a rodent's life— scampering up hillsides under cover of darkness, finding holes to crawl into when daylight broke, carrying on their backs 4-kg backpacks that held sleeping bags, extra pairs of socks, shaving kits and letters from home. They would nibble on hard, stale puris when hunger struck. Though the nala was close, with its fresh water beckoning, they could never reach it because the enemy would fire from the top. Instead, they would reach into crevices to snap off icicles that they would suck greedily on to quench their thirst. They would fill their water bottles with crushed snow for the endless rocky climbs where water would not be found and crack icicles under their teeth, swirling them around in their mouths like the coloured iced lollies from their childhood. When Manoj returned to his trench after a taxing assignment, bone-tired and shivering, and closed his eyes for a few moments of respite, images that were hidden in some corner of his mind, carefully wrapped in the cobwebs of time, came back to haunt him.

———

'Bhaiya kuch toh le lo,' (Brother, take something, at least) the three-year-old could hear his mother's voice from somewhere in the distance. His eyes were lost in the cacophony of sound and colour that play an important part in the wooing ritual of young innocents by the habitual seducers, big cities.

It was his first visit to Lucknow and the little boy from Rudha village, dressed in his best khaki shorts and cotton shirt, was looking with wide-eyed wonder at the new world unfolding before him. He had never beheld these sights before. Around him there were hawkers selling sticks of fluffy pink candyfloss and bright-orange bars of ice-cream;

crisp golgappas were disappearing into open mouths, and on a wooden cart, a man was grating ice to a fine powder that he would collect in a mud bowl, sprinkle with some bright red syrup, stick a wooden spoon into and hand over to outstretched arms.

He felt his mother pull on his little hand and suddenly his senses were assaulted by a big man with a ferocious black upturned moustache and yellow paan-stained teeth that flashed in his face when he parted his lips in a big smile. Behind him, on a wooden pole, were tied balloons and bright plastic toys—pistols with brown butts, squeaky green parrots with shiny red beaks, catapults, whistles and dolls.

What caught his eye was a brown wooden flute, dotted with darker stains. 'I want that,' he told his mother. She tried to tempt him to buy a toy since she felt he would not be able to play it but he was undeterred. Finally, she gave up and paying Rs 2 to the vendor, placed the flute in her son's little hand, quite sure that he would throw it away before the day ended.

She was wrong. The flute stayed with Manoj for the next 21 years. He would take it out every day, play a tune on it and then place it back in his cupboard next to his neatly folded clothes.

Even when he went away, first to Sainik School, then the National Defence Academy (NDA) and finally, the snow-clad peaks of Kargil, the flute would remain in his trunk of old clothes and memories that his mother would eventually stop looking at because it always made her cry.

Deep in his stomach, Manoj could feel a faint rumble. He wondered if the man beside him could hear it, too. Hunger pangs were striking. There was an cold puri lying in his backpack somewhere, but he didn't care much for it. It was like chewing on cardboard. This time it was his tongue that tempted his mind to go back to the mess where dosa, sambhar and that spicy chutney called gunpowder would be served on Sunday afternoons for brunch. 'Gunpowder,' he said aloud and laughed dryly. His mind went back to that first Sunday in the regiment when the commanding officer (CO) had asked him for a glass of wine. A teetotaller, and new to the Army then, he didn't know how wine was served and summoning the mess waiter had naively asked: 'How will you have it, Sir? With soda or water?' The bar had rung out with amused laughter.

Manoj shook his head to shake the memories out of it and concentrated on the task ahead: He and his men had been climbing in miserable darkness for almost nine hours. Most of them had rolled up their jackets and shoved them into their backpacks. Manoj had a pair of spare woollen socks that he had wrapped around the breechblock of his rifle to keep it warm and lubricated and protected against jamming in the cold. A seized weapon in war could make the difference between life and death. On the last mission, a man's breechblock had jammed and he had had to hastily light a precious fuel tablet under it to get it back in working order. He didn't want that happening tonight.

Though the night temperature was touching sub-zero, the arduous climb made the soldiers sweat. Manoj led his men, quick and noiseless. He would slip his fingers into cracks in the rocks and pull himself up, feeling his way ahead, deliberately keeping his mind off the fact that there could be a snake or a scorpion sitting in a crevice, ready to strike. The ascent was slow and nerve-wracking. Besides the terrain and the bad weather, there was the constant trepidation that the very next fold in the ridge could be an enemy hideout or a bunker. Every still shadow in a crevice appeared to be a Pathan lurking with a gun. The fear was constant, dogging them at every step, constricting their throats with its suffocating grip, making goosebumps erupt on their cold, wet skin.

Climbing was a thirst-inducing business and most of the men had finished their one-litre water bottles. They found some patches of snow under larger stones. While some of it was fresh and could be picked up in greedy fistfuls to quench thirst, most of it was too contaminated by gunpowder to be of any use. Manoj ran his tongue over chapped lips and didn't reach for water even though he was tempted. There was just one last sip left. He wanted it there for psychological support till the end.

His thoughts went to his mother and lingered lovingly over there. He saw her, brow-lined with worry, gentle and caring in her faded green cotton sari, leaning forward to kiss his forehead softly as he told her stories of Siachen from where he had just returned. He blinked the moisture out of his eyes.

As often happens with children who have grown up in humble circumstances, Manoj had always been a careful spender. His father ran a small hosiery business and had a family of three sons and a daughter to bring up. Being the eldest son, his parents' efforts to make ends meet were never hidden from the quiet child, who spoke little but observed a lot from underneath dark eyelashes that were always bent over a course book. He was an outstanding student right from the beginning. He knew he had to do well in life so that the future could give his family all the happiness they couldn't afford right now. He wouldn't ask for new clothes till the old ones started showing tears that could not be darned anymore; whatever he had would be neatly folded and put back in the cupboard. His books, with brown covers, would be put back into his school bag after every use, his notebooks would be filled with his neat and steady handwriting, with its delicate right slant, just the way his Montessori school teacher had told him to write; his copies would never have an ink stain or an untidy scribble running across the page. Manoj knew money was short, he knew the value of each hard-earned rupee. He understood just how difficult it was to get a family two square meals a day, just how tough it was to keep hunger at bay.

The train had slowly started moving out of Jhansi railway station. Suddenly a dark, ugly, wrinkled face thrust itself at him from behind the iron rails of the window. A pair of dull eyes, hazy with cataract, looked greedily at the shiny silver-foiled paper plate of food he was holding. A dirty hand shot forth and gestured towards a hollow stomach, with dark folds of scaly skin hanging over the edges of a faded petticoat. 'Bhook lagi hai beta,' (I am hungry, son) the withered old woman grovelled, her grey hair falling untidily over her face.

Before his father could reach into his wallet for some change, Manoj had put his hand out between the bars and handed her the steaming hot plate of chole bhature. The train picked up speed and chugged out of the platform; the old lady was left behind holding a full meal in her calloused old hands.

Since he hadn't been well, Manoj hadn't eaten for a day after his passing-out parade at NDA and his father had got down at Jhansi to get him something to eat. When his mother scolded him for giving the food away he had told her affectionately that he was a strong young man and could stay hungry for two days but the old woman needed to eat.

The men had been climbing for more than fourteen hours. They hadn't slept for twenty-four. Sudden downpours of sleet and snow had left them chilled to the bone. They had miscalculated the treacherous path, lost their way twice in the dark and it was already morning by the time they spotted the hazy outline of the top.

They had the option to go back before the enemy spotted them but Manoj made up his mind—they would complete the task they had been sent for. There would be any turning back now. They would storm the enemy bunkers, making the best of the bad weather and the wet mist creeping up the cliffs, with its cold fingers on all it found in its path.

Another volley of fire lit up the sky. Manoj knew the guns were lined up on the highway, all along the Indus, firing at least 20,000 rounds at a time. The aim was to distract the enemy, which was why he and his men had been able to climb the 70-degree incline unnoticed do far. However, this time the fire seemed to be coming dangerously close. The burst of the shells was accompanied by a hail of bullets and suddenly a soldier screamed out in pain and collapsed.

'Take cover,' Manoj shouted, 'this looks like enemy fire.' The bullets, rockets and machinegun fire were coming at them with an unnerving accuracy. The cries of men who had been hit rang out through the stillness of the chilly morning.

From behind the boulder where he had taken cover, Manoj looked out. Around him was death and destruction. Limbs had been torn apart, flesh ripped into, and blood was seeping into the soil as the gut-wrenching screams of his men echoed in the impersonal stillness of the bare brown mountains.

He knew they would have to storm the enemy in a daring daylight attack, right now. As soon as him mind was made up, the rush of adrenaline overcame indecision, fear and nervousness. The paralysing cold seeping into his bones was replaced by the heat of blood coursing through his veins. As the tracer bullet came flying past, lighting the place with a deadly cocktail of shrapnel and fire, Manoj stood up, tall and brave, his slight frame coiled like spring, his face a mask. Through the scream of the wind, he roared at those of his men that were fit to fight, ordering them to follow him through the hail of bullets. Like a colossal god with invincible powers he walked into the curtain of shells and bullets. He didn't look back even once to see who had followed his final command but if he had he would have been a satisfied man. All his Gorkha jawans who could pick themselves up and walk were right behind him, their khukris gripped firmly in their hands.

Leaving behind those dead or dying, the men charged like angry lions, placing their feet firmly on the sleet-covered jagged rocks, following the man, who was not walking through flying bullets for the first time. They had seen him do it before. Just about a month ago.

About a month back

In a narrow gulley, the bodies of four men from an ambushed patrol had been lying for more than 10 days since the Kargil War had started. They were from an initial patrol that had been sent to reconnoitre the occupied heights when the Indian Army had grossly underestimated the enemy infiltration. Completely unaware that they were being watched by the Pakistanis from both sides of the gulley, the men had walked into a deadly trap. They were shot dead at point-blank range by enemy soldiers sitting at a height on both sides. All efforts to retrieve the bodies were repulsed by the Pakistanis, who would start firing indiscriminately the moment they spotted any activity from the Indian side.

Manoj volunteered to go and get the dead men back, insisting that their bodies be wrapped in the Tricolour and sent home to their families. He and his men had crept behind boulders and climbed the heights, reaching higher than the enemy. Then while some men were engaged in firing, the officer and a few of his men crawled down to where the bodies were lying, and ignoring the hail of bullets flying past, dragged the bullet-riddled bodies out of the gulley.

Manoj had been one of the first to reach and had boldly crawled up to a dead man, pulling him behind a boulder. For a moment, he had stopped to look at his dead mate and his heart burned with rage. The body was badly mangled by shrapnel and he couldn't make out the man's face. On his bloody finger there was a gold ring that told him the man had probably been married. Even the belt he wore around his waist was punctured with bullet holes.

'You bloody dogs, I'll throw you out of my country,' he had promised the enemy, shouting out in anger and had then used all his strength to drag the dead soldier back.

It was a miraculous retrieval and even a decade later officers who had watched the operation would sit with a glass of whiskey in the mess and remember the amazing man who had managed the impossible. 'It needed a very big heart to do what he did,' they would say. 'Only he could have done it.'

The time has come to show that daring once again and Manoj does not disappoint his men. Adrenaline coursing through his veins, he gestures to them to follow and, steeling his heart against every instinct for self-preservation, walks into the curtain of flying bullets to reach the first bunker on the ridge—a pile of cut rocks with a boulder for a roof, grainy in the brooding fog that is sweeping across the landscape. He can make out the shadowy outlines of two Pakistani Northern Light Infantry soldiers. He is not conscious of an effort but a sharp tug at his belt apprises him

*that his hand has gripped the handle of the khukri hanging there
and whipped it out in a silken move. The sheath falls away limply
by his side as his hand flashes its ferocious blade up in the chilly
wind. The thumping of his heart is left behind in an instant as
he runs across the uneven terrain, jumping over boulders in the
falling snow, his face a grotesque mask of death, and falls upon
the enemy soldiers, ferocious and proud. There is a swish in the
air as the blade, cutting through the falling snowflakes, flashes
and slices into human flesh.*

*Right to left, left to right. Then again. And again. The bodies
of the shocked Pakistanis, terror written in their eyes, fall in a
bloody pile. They could have never imagined that someone would
walk in through the deadly fire. Had he been watching, the young
officer's regimental centre khukri ustad would be proud of his
student as he lets the blood drip off his khukri and looks up to
find his next target.*

*Sprinting across to the second bunker, the men fiercely pounce
upon the enemy and a bloody hand-to-hand combat follows, 'Jai
Mahakali, Aayo Gorkhali' piercing the cold morning. Return
shots ring out. Some of the enemy soldiers are charging with their
bayonets, but most find they are no match for the gutsy Gorkhas
with their lethal khukris that are splashing blood on the wet
rocks. Suddenly Manoj winces. He has been hit in the shoulder
by a bullet. Unconcerned, and feeling no pain in the heat of the
moment, he takes out his gun and moves on to the next bunker,
spraying the ones hiding there with a shower of bullets.*

*Another bullet comes and hits him in the leg, making him
stagger unsteadily. 'Naa chodnu,' (Don't leave them) he cries out
in Gorkhali, telling his men to carry on the carnage, and drags
his injured leg forward. Reaching out for a grenade, he lobs it*

at the fourth bunker from where mortar fire is coming at them. Even as an explosion rents the sky, throwing up a dull grey cloud of stone and debris, a fatal shot bursts through the air and hits the officer in the forehead. There is a flash of yellow and he is engulfed by the smell of burning cordite and a warmth in the freezing cold. His whole body is wracked by a terrible pain; his brain is on fire, his lungs gasping for breath, his heart seems to want to force itself out of his chest and his tongue is dry and swollen with thirst. He wants to go on and shoot the Pakistani soldier he can see leaping out of the burning bunker and race down the slope, but his disobedient body had stopped listening to his commands. He can only watch as his arms let go of the rifle he has been holding, his fingers lose their grip on the trigger, his knees buckle under him and his neck slumps forward on his heaving chest. Blood courses down his face, blurring his vision. There is a spurt of light in his head, then stark darkness and silence. Finally, he has to close his eyes.

Manoj Kumar Pandey of 1/11 Gorkha Rifles is dead; his blood-stained body tilts in an arch and falls gently to the ground in front of the fourth bunker of Khalubar. He is 24 years and seven days old.

About six years ago . . .

On a warm, sultry summer afternoon, a thin boy with a side parting in his hair and shiny new leather shoes walked down for his service selection board interview for NDA. He was trying to keep his mind off the bite in his toes, the sting of the cheap elastic in his socks and the guilt he had felt asking his poor father for money to buy them. He reminded himself that he was the best NCC cadet in his state and desperately hoped that his basic knowledge of English would not desert him during the interview.

'Why do you want to join the Army?' the interviewing officer was stern and abrupt, and looking straight into his eyes.

'I want to win the Param Vir Chakra,' he replied returning the stare, hoping the sentence was grammatically correct. The interviewing officer looked at the others on the board and exchanged a smile.

Sometimes, they say, there is magic in the air and we must be careful about what we say because it will come true. Not only did young Manoj Kumar Pandey from Sitapur district in Uttar Pradesh get into NDA, he also won the Param Vir Chakra, the Armed Forces' highest gallantry award. Unfortunately, he hadn't said he wanted to wear it live.

Yogender Singh Yadav

Grenadier Yogender Singh Yadav was lying in a pile of bodies. Around him lay his comrades, all six of them, brutally killed. Their fingers had been ripped off, limbs torn out of their bodies, legs twisted grotesquely under their torsos, heads smashed beyond recognition.

War is terrible. It reduces breathing, living, brave, young men into lumps of bloody flesh and bone. It reduces friends, colleagues, brothers, fathers and husbands into scarred, broken, ragdolls that were indistinguishable from each other, their vacant dead eyes mute witness to the pain they had undergone. It also reduces soldiers, trained emotionless killing machines, to emotional wrecks.

When Yogender Singh tried to stand up his leg just collapsed under him and he lay there and wept, the sound of his loud wailing echoing in the cold, desolate heights of Tiger

Hill. He wept till his eyes ran dry and his throat didn't have the strength for another cry. He didn't know then, but there were fourteen bullets lodged in his body. Six of them had cut into his arm, rendering it useless as it hung from the shoulder, the bones exposed and rubbing painfully against each other each time he shifted his weight. A grenade had burst at his foot, making him feel as if his leg had been cut off—he could not feel it anymore. Another had smashed across his face, slicing into his forehead leaving a gaping gash from where blood was dripping into his eyes.

It was all over, he thought.

———

When the Kargil War started, Yogender Singh Yadav had been on leave. It had barely been a fortnight since he had married Reena, and her pretty, smiling face was still on his mind when he joined his battalion in Dras on 22 May. That very day they had their first casualty. The reality of war dawned on Yogender Singh during his initial deployment as a fighting porter when, in 22 days, he witnessed the loss of two officers, two JCOs (junior commissioned officers) and 21 soldiers.

After the capture of Tololing by 2 Raj. Rif. (Rajputana Rifles) and 13 JAK Rif. (Jammu and Kashmir Rifles), Yogender's battalion was withdrawn to Ghumri where they spent a few days recouping and repairing equipment. Within four days, they got orders to attack Tiger Hill, which was the highest peak of the Dras area. The Pakistanis had set up bunkers there. Colonel Kushal Chand Thakur, commanding officer of the battalion, had a darbar and briefed the men about the task at hand. He told them that they were fortunate to be getting an opportunity to take revenge for the deaths of the men they had lost. Standing in the cold, he pointed out to them the post they had to attack.

Ghatak Platoon, the commando section of the battalion, would be the first to attack. Yogender Singh Yadav was not in the Ghatak Platoon, but since men were needed to fill up for those who had died in Tololing, he was one of the chosen few. 'There were 23 of us,' he says, 'one officer, one JCO and 21 jawans. I looked up to where CO Saab was pointing and I could see a straight rock-face rising into the sky. It would be a difficult climb, I thought, but we would do it.' The men would soon discover that not only was the route difficult, it also had enemy posts on either side. And not only would they have to dodge enemy fire, the precarious height would cause breathing problems, the lack of proper winter clothing would be a major deterrent and the cold would seep right into their bones.

2–3 June 1999

It was a dark night. Led by Captain Sachin Nimbalkar and Lieutenant Balwan, the men climbed in silence. No one seemed to want to break the quiet, particularly because they didn't know how long it would last. Using hands and feet and ropes to pull each other up, they climbed higher and higher on Tiger Hill, shadowy figures that appeared like ghosts of the night. It was becoming colder with each step and the men were badly missing the winter clothing that hadn't reached them yet. Most of them were in combat gear with sweaters and jackets; they had their own gloves and boots, but these could not compare with the comfort of snow shoes and gloves. The reinforcements would arrive only after 18 Grenadiers had captured Tiger Hill, but for these men of Ghatak Platoon and Delta Company who were tasked with attack and support that would be too late.

It was only when morning broke that the men realized that they had been climbing through the night. Taking cover behind rocks, they waited to assess the situation. In their backpacks were rations for 72 hours—dry puris, cashew nuts, raisins, almonds, tea leaves and milk powder. Some men had bought biscuits from the last village they had crossed, so they were richer than others.

Just ahead rose a crest that Capt. Nimbalkar felt was Tiger Hill. The men decided to keep walking and were disappointed to reach there at 5.30 a.m. only to find that it was a false crest. They climbed down and kept walking. The entire day passed and hunger pangs began to hit them, but the men did not stop.

At around 6 p.m., they had almost reached the top. Capt. Nimbalkar asked the Ghatak Platoon to take a break and make tea while he and a few other soldiers would go and reconnoitre the area. It appeared calm and silent and Nimbalkar and his boys had just moved about 100 metres ahead when they were suddenly hit by a volley of fire. They had walked right on to a ridge that had enemy bunkers on both sides.

Taking shelter behind rocks they called for help. The men opened fire, but it was completely ineffective since they could only see the fire coming, but not where the Pakistanis were. The tea break was quickly given up and the CO informed about the setback over the wireless set. They were told to stay behind the rocks and keep their heads down—the Army would give them artillery support. The guns started firing from Dras and finally by midnight the men were rescued. They were miraculously unhurt except for one soldier who had injured his hand.

Now that their cover had broken and the Pakistanis knew that Indian soldiers were already on Tiger Hill, CO Kushal Thakur directed the men to attack before the enemy could react. When it came to choosing between life and food, food again took a backseat and all plans for a meal were dropped again. The men got on their feet and, with Yogender Singh Yadav and his namesake Yogendra Yadav leading as scout number one and two, they started climbing again. At 5.30 a.m. when they were in a nala, climbing up via a narrow bridge with water trickling under their feet, they were suddenly hit by gunfire. It was coming from enemy bunkers lined up on both sides of the ridge.

There was complete chaos and only the seven soldiers who were right in front managed to climb up, the rest cut off by the fire and forced to step back. Yogender Singh Yadav, his buddy Yogendra Yadav, and five other soldiers had managed to cross the enemy fire. However, they had been cut off from the rest of their comrades. They had no option, but to go ahead on their own.

A terrible adventure was in store for them.

———

Yogender's story

There were just seven of us now and we could not even turn back since the enemy had cut off our route. We decided to go on. Right ahead we could see a post. It was a rough sangar (a small, temporary fortified position originally made up of stone, now built of sandbags and similar materials) made of rocks piled up together. We had no idea how many of them were inside it, but since we had seen them before they saw us, we just opened fire on them.

Four of their men were killed instantly. When they stopped firing, we knew they had all died. By then, alerted by the exchange of gunfire, the Pakistani soldiers in another bunker above us had started shooting at us as well. It was a Catch-22 situation. Bullets were flying through the air and we could neither go back nor forward.

Just then, Havaldar Madan, who was our team leader, shouted, 'Get inside their sangar. That is the only safe place.' Someone shouted back that the area could be mined but Hav. Madan said there was no choice. 'Pehle goliyon se bacho phir mines ke baare mein sochna,' (First, take cover from the bullets, then think of mines) he said curtly and we made a dash for the sangar. They had not had the time to mine it. Once inside, we took up firing positions and, with the bodies of the dead Pakistanis lying around us, opened fire on the bunker above us.

The shootout went on for five long hours. There were no casualties, but the constant fire did not allow us to advance an inch. We realized that with all reinforcements cut off from below, our ammunition would not last very long. The ammunition left behind by the dead Pakistanis was also being used up fast. It was just a matter of time before we ran out of bullets. We thought we would die and decided we would kill as many as we could before getting killed. So, we decided to stop firing and let them get closer.

Around 11.30 a.m., 12 enemy soldiers came down to check if we were dead or alive. We still had 45 rounds each in our rifles and were just lying low. They came really close. I still remember them clearly, they were in cream-coloured Pathani suits with yellow pagris and had flowing beards. They were wearing white coats with hoods. Some of them were really tall while others were of medium height.

We kept quiet till they came really close. Then suddenly all seven of us opened fire at them. Except for two enemy soldiers, who managed to escape, all the others were killed. The survivors ran up to their other post and within half an hour, more than 35 Pakistani jawans had surrounded us. The sound of gunfire echoed through the peaks as they directed the fire of their heavy weapons at us. We were facing HMG (heavy machine gun), UMG (uber machine gun) and RPG (rocket-propelled grenade) rounds that were flying at the sangar from the top. They also started rolling large boulders down at us.

Since there was very limited ammunition with us, we did not want to waste any and stopped firing. They spotted our light machine gun and directed RPG fire at it, blasting its barrel off. A young soldier was manning it and he ran to Hav. Madan in panic. Hav. Madan asked me to throw the LMG in his direction. Just as I went to pick it up, I looked up and found seven men in Pathani suits standing right above the sangar. 'Ustad, woh aa gaye hain,' (they are here) I shouted to Hav. Madan. Ustad told me and Grenadier Ananth Ram to go and support our sniper Lance Naik Naresh. The moment I ran to do that, they flung a grenade at me. It hit me in the knee; it felt as if my leg had been blasted off. I felt it with my hand and was relieved to find it still there. Just then, another grenade caught me on the forehead. I collapsed, blinded by pain and the blood that was dripping into my eyes from the deep gash. It was flowing like water from an open tap. I couldn't see a thing.

By then, both Grenadier Ananth and I had reached Lance Naik Naresh, the sniper we had been told to help. I asked Naresh to bandage my head since the blood was flowing into my eyes but he told me to start firing first. I kept wiping the blood off my face with an old sleeping bag that was lying there. Seeing my plight, Naresh opened his roll of bandage. As he was trying to put it on my wound, a shell hit him. He closed his eyes, leaned back and fell down. He was dead with the bandage still in his hand.

I turned to Ananth and had only just started telling him this when a UMG burst hit him too. His head was blown off. After that there was complete pandemonium. One after the other, the Pakistanis jumped down on us with cries of 'Allah hu Akbar'. There must have been around 35 of them with weapons in their hands. Out of the seven of us, two were dead, two were injured (including me and the other Yogendra whose finger had been cut off). So there were just three functional men facing 35 heavily armed enemy soldiers.

In a second even that would change.

———

All of Yadav's mates were killed in the machine gun fire that the Pakistani soldiers directed at them. They were so heavily outnumbered that they did not get a chance to retaliate.

Yogender Singh Yadav was the only one who did not die despite the Pakistanis making every effort to ensure that there were no survivors by firing at the fallen men again and again. When four rounds were fired at the man next to him, Yogender Singh Yadav saw his body shudder and jump in the air. He just closed his eyes and waited for his own turn to be killed. A Pakistani soldier came close and fired at him even as he lay there with his eyes shut. Yogender Singh felt the bullets hitting his body, but he promised himself that he would not die.

Satisfied that all the Indian soldiers had been killed, the Pakistanis sent a message to their base camp in the Mushkoh valley that there were Indian soldiers on the mountain and an Indian LMG post down below that should be destroyed. Yogender Singh knew that 18 of the soldiers, who had split up from his team, were trapped on the mountain. An overwhelming desire to stay alive if only to save their lives came over him and he willed himself to not lose consciousness.

Through his bloodied eyes, he could faintly see two men coming in his direction. One of them picked up his gun, not realizing that he had a hand grenade strapped to his beLt Using all his remaining strength, Yogender Singh Yadav pulled out the grenade, removed the pin and flung it at the retreating Pakistani soldier. It got stuck in the hood of his jacket and though he tried to throw it off, it was too late. An explosion rent the air and the Pakistani's head was blown off. He dropped down dead right on top of Yadav. Yogender Singh Yadav picked up his rifle and though he could not stand, he started shooting the other enemy soldiers who were standing a little distance away.

The shooting created instant panic. The Pakistanis, who had believed that all the Indians were dead, thought reinforcements had arrived from below and panicked. As they ran, Yogender Singh Yadav crawled after them and saw their camp. 'It was 1.30 p.m., the sun was out and I could clearly see snow tents and a langar (meal) in progress. I couldn't do anything since I wasn't even able to stand, but I had this mad desire to survive and go down to my MMG (medium machine gun) post to warn my battalion.'

As he crawled back to where his comrades lay dead, Yogender Singh looked at them. 'Someone had his head blown off, someone had a ripped chest, someone's intestines were falling out of a sliced stomach. These were my friends; they had been closer to me than my own brothers. Everybody had died a painful death except me. I just sat there and cried. And cried,' he says.

As his body started getting cold, he started feeling the intense pain of his terrible injuries. His shoulder bones had become exposed and were rubbing against each other making him cry out each time he shifted he moved. He realized his arm had become useless. After unsuccessfully trying to pull it out of the shoulder socket, he just pushed it on his back and tucked it inside his belt so that it would not come in the way.

'Inside my head I heard a voice saying, if you are not dead yet, you will not die now. And then it said get inside the nala,' says Yogendra. And then, with his shattered arm tucked into his belt and with fifteen bullets in his body, Yogender Singh crawled into a nala near the sangar and slowly dropped down into it.

5 June

Yadav was hanging from a rock with his good hand when he saw the rest of the 18 Grenadiers party down below. Calling out to them, he asked for help. The men quickly got him down and, taking turns to carry him on their backs, they brought him to the camp that had been established midway on Tiger Hill. The sun had set by the time a weak and shivering Yogender Singh Yadav was brought to the CO's tent. The immense blood loss had made him so weak that he could no longer see. Yet, when his CO asked him if he could recognize him, Yogender Singh Yadav said, 'Saab mein aapki awaz pehchanta hun. Jai Hind, Saab!' (Sir, I recognize your voice. Jai Hind, Sir!)

Lying down in the CO's tent, warmed by stoves that were lit up to stop his constant shivering, Yogender Singh Yadav told his battalion exactly where the enemy was, how their post could be reached and what route should be followed. He then passed out.

Three days later

Yogender Singh Yadav recovered consciousness on 9 July. It had been three days since he had been shifted from Tiger

Hill to the Base Hospital at Srinagar. He woke up to find a ceiling fan above him and, for a moment, could not figure out where he was. The nurse informed him that he was out of danger and in the hospital. He asked about his battalion and was told that Tiger Hill had been attacked by around 100 soldiers of Bravo and Delta Companies along with Ghatak the night that he had returned. They had followed his advise and had taken over the post without any resistance from the enemy. Almost two truckloads of ammunition were recovered from Tiger Hill. The haul included a .82 mortar.

Yogender Singh Yadav was shifted to Delhi where bone grafting was done on his arm. He was lucky that all the bullets had missed his vital organs and, though it took many years to recover fully, he now bears only bullet scars and/the cut on his abdomen from where ribs were taken for bone grafting. His arm hurts in the winter and he can't lift it beyond a certain height, but Yogender Singh Yadav has accepted that gracefully. Looking at him, it is hard to believe that he shot five men in cold blood, held his own against a company-strength of Pakistani soldiers and nearly died on a craggy peak.

Every Republic Day, he comes down to Delhi, puts on his number one uniform, pins his medals on his chest and leads the parade down Rajpath from an open jeep with the other two living PVCs—Capt. Bana Singh and Hav. Sanjay Kumar—by his side.

How does it feel to see thousands of fellow citizens cheering for him? 'I feel humbled and grateful,' he says. 'I am a soldier, it was my job to fight yet, I have been decorated with the highest gallantry award of my country for completing a task that was given to me. Any soldier would have done the same.'

Yogender Singh Yadav was born in Aurangabad Ahir village near Bulandshahr in Uttar Pradesh. The village has a population of 5000; its farmers grow wheat and sugar cane. Yogender's father, Mr Ram Karan Singh, was an ex-serviceman, serving with 11 Kumaon as a soldier and even participating in the 1971 War. After eight years, he took premature retirement and came back to live in his village. He would often tell Yogender Singh and his two brothers stories about the war, inspiring them to join the Army.

Yogender Singh began his education at the village primary school and, after class 5, joined Sannota Sri Krishna College, which was about 3 km from his home. Halfway through his class 12, when he was just 16 years old, Yogender Singh was recruited into the Army. He was 19 when he went to fight in Kargil. The Param Vir Chakra was announced for Yadav posthumously, but it was soon discovered that he was recuperating in a hospital, and it was his namesake, who had been killed in the mission.

Based on a narration by Subedar Yogender Singh Yadav, PVC.

Sanjay Kumar

In the tidy olive-green Army cantonment in Dehradun where 13 Jammu and Kashmir Rifles (JAK Rif.) is stationed, soldiers sleep after a long, tiring day of training. The alarm in most barracks goes off at 5 a.m. on weekdays; it rings in the room Havaldar Sanjay Kumar shares with his buddy Lance Naik Sandip.

After a mug of hot chai, the soldiers are on the PT ground by 6 a.m., ready for their daily 5-km run. A breakfast of puri-sabzi or ande ki bhujia in the langar, when they crack jokes or discuss the latest political developments or a film, and they return to their barracks for a bath and change of clothes.

Little separates Sanjay Kumar from the other men. But when he buttons up his uniform his eye goes to the small ribbon dangling from his chest with the other service ribbons—a small ceremonial medal that only three living people in the entire Armed Forces wear, the Param Vir Chakra. Sanjay Kumar has been wearing the highest gallantry award of free India for 14 years.

Area Flat Top, Point 4875
4 July 1999, 1 p.m.

The searing heat from the enemy machine gun reaches 23-year-old Sanjay Kumar's freezing face. For a moment, he relaxes in its warmth. He hasn't slept for 30 hours; he has been climbing for 18 hours, and tiredness and cold have seeped down to his bones. The temptation to lean back and shut his eyes is tremendous, but he resists. Instead, he reaches into his backpack and pulls out a roll of white gauze bandage from his first-aid kit. He wraps it around his hands, systematically and meticulously—turning his attention to the left first and then the right. There isn't enough for both and he looks at his comrade—Rifleman Najinder Singh, who is leaning back on the rock by his side, face covered with grime, eyes red from lack of sleep, hands lacerated from the sharp rocks he has held to climb through the night. Najinder moves the grenade he is holding to his left hand and reaches into his backpack. Wordlessly, he hands over his own bandage-roll to his mate. Holding one end in his mouth, Sanjay carefully wraps the rest around his right hand. Taking the roll in clockwise circles, he covers his fingers first. Only when he is satisfied that the padding is thick enough will he move on to cover his thumb.

The Pakistanis, sitting in an open sangar (a small, temporary fortified position) at Area Flat Top, Pt. 4875, with their machineguns firing down the slope, are under the impression that the Indian Army squad is still climbing up the steep 70-degree incline. They are mistaken. One JCO (junior commissioned officer) and 10 other ranks of Charlie Company, 13 JAK Rif., have already reached them and are now sitting behind boulders just a few feet below their sangar. Riflemen Sanjay Kumar and Najinder Singh are the first two men of that attack squad. They are the scouts.

Sanjay has finished bandaging his hands. They look like the fat white stumps now. He takes a deep breath and his eyes met Najinder's one last time. The moment is here.

The night of 3–4 July
The climb

The men had eaten a hot meal of dal, chawal and sabzi. Some time earlier they had attended the havan and puja held by the unit pandit and now, with shoes laced on, helmets pulled down over their heads, red tilaks on their foreheads and bits of prasad still between their teeth, they were ready for the assault on Flat top feature of Pt. 4875.

The sun was setting over the jagged peaks around Mushkoh valley. The temperature had dropped a few more degrees and the chilling wind was screaming in their ears when the 60 men of Charlie Company, under their company commander Major Gurpreet Singh, began their long climb. Around the same time, another team of soldiers from 17 Jat had also started up. Their task was to recapture the peaks—Pimple

1 and Pimple 2 and Area Flat Top on Pt. 4875. Though the two parties could not see each other, they were in radio communication. The plan was that the men would climb through the night and reach the top by 3 a.m. There they would launch simultaneous attacks on all three points while still under cover of darkness, clear the area of enemy soldiers and bring it back under Indian control.

Artillery guns along the base of Mushkoh valley had already started pounding the three points with near continuous shelling. The guns were deployed to engage the enemy so that the soldiers climbing up would have minimum casualties. Though the guns caused great losses they also warned the Pakistanis of an attack night and the climbing men were not surprised when they ran into a volley of machine gun fire coming from the top.

Rifleman Kuldeep Singh was the first to be hit. He screamed and fell, bleeding. While he was being evacuated, the rest of the men sat under the cover of rocks. Since the enemy was firing at all paths within its sight, it was decided that the only way to climb unnoticed was via the steep rock face right under Pt. 4875, the only path not visible from the top. But there was a hitch—there was no route, just a steep vertical line up of jagged rocks glinting in the moonlight.

Getting up quickly and standing on the edge of their toes to heave themselves up, the soldiers started pulling themselves up the incline one by one, using their hands to find a grip on the sharp rocks that had to support their body weight. The better climbers went first with picks and ropes and dropped a line for the ones following in the darkness. One wrong step could send them plunging to their death in the gaping valley.

It was best that they could not see the sheer drop below because they could have lost their nerve. Blind to the risk, they worked their way up, gasping under the effort of pulling their body weight up those deadly heights, taking short breaks to catch their breath and distracting their minds from the gruesome task ahead by watching the Bofors shots whistling above their heads and smashing on the rocks.

The next morning

The darkness was slowly peeling away under the lukewarm rays of the rising sun. The men had climbed through the night but were still 250 m from Area Flat Top and now visible to the Pakistani soldiers on Pimple 1 and Pimple 2, who had started firing at them. The soldiers of 17 Jat were facing the same problem. While they were not visible from Pimple 1 and 2 (the heights they were climbing), the enemy at Pt. 4875 could see them and had opened crossfire on them.

The 13 JAK Rif. took shelter behind South Spur, a small hump where they were protected from the fire. But they were still 150 m from the first enemy position and under continuous machinegun fire. The enemy's guns would stop firing only for about a minute—each time a rocket launcher hit their sangar and the soldiers went down to shelter from the deadly rock splintering around them. It was decided that the Indian team would take advantage of that one-minute lull; a leading section of one JCO and 10 other ranks would cover the 150 m running to reach the enemy position. Rifleman

Sanjay Kumar and Rifleman Najinder volunteered to lead.

The next time a shell hit Pt. 4875 and the enemy machine guns stopped firing for a minute, the two soldiers ran across the jagged rock-face, guns in hand. When the enemy soldiers re-emerged from their bunker, they had no idea that the Indians were already sitting a few feet away, waiting for an opportune moment to attack. Crouched right under the enemy bunker, Sanjay Kumar and Najinder Singh could feel their own hearts beat. Over their heads, there were two enemy machine guns shooting almost continuously. If Sanjay wanted he could stretch an arm and touch either, he thought. And that was how the fantastic idea came to him.

———

Sanjay makes eye contact with Najinder and nods. Najinder pulls the pin from the grenade in his hand and, with his arm arching in a slow semi-circle, lobs it inside the enemy bunker. There is an evil hiss, a blast, the familiar smell of cordite and then cries of pain as the bunker erupts in the grey foggy afternoon.

Sanjay keeps his head down until the sharp rocks around him have stopped splintering. His face an emotionless mask, he reaches out for the enemy machinegun closest to him and with his bandaged hands protecting him from the burning metal, he pulls it down and flings it on the rocks below. He then turns to the second gun. Najinder Singh notices that the bandages around Sanjay's hands have started smoking and are coiling around his fingers like twisted black snakes but Sanjay is oblivious. He reaches for his AK-47, whips it off his shoulder and turns it into the gap from where he has pulled out the guns. Three Pakistani soldiers are standing in the smoke-filled sangar, paralysed by fear and shock. Around them lie guns, grenades and a large stock of ammunition. From the corner of his eye, he spots half-a-dozen bodies piled up at the other end. One of the men is trying to reach for a gun. Sanjay presses the trigger. A volley of gunfire dances across, splattering the rocks with a spray of warm blood, and the three men who had manned the first sangar of Pt. 4875 drop down one after the other.

The soldier with the soot-covered fingers keeps firing and only after he is convinced that the men are all dead does he look at his grubby hands and wipes them on his dirty, threadbare trouser front. Fourteen years later, he will very humbly tell a writer that there was no special bravery involved. He was just doing what any other soldier in his place would have done under the circumstances. He would wear the PVC ribbon proudly on his uniform, but be embarrassed by the attention it brought him, insisting that every single soldier in his attack team was as brave as he was. Yet he would wear a medal that very few people have worn live so far. A medal that even the Chief of Army Staff gets up to salute. Even if it hangs on the shirtfront of a 23-year-old foot soldier.

———

After the Indian soldiers have taken over the first sangar, they move to the second. They are unaware that, anticipating an attack, the enemy soldiers have climbed out of their bunker and have taken up positions further up the mountain from where they will target the Indians at point-blank range. All of the Indians are shot at. Two of them will never rise again. Naib Subedar

Ramesh Singh survives but he is not destined to live long. He will come back alive but meet his end in Kashmir soon after. Sanjay Kumar is the one who embraces life despite three bullets in his leg and two in his hip. He and his surviving comrades lie back on the rocks and pretend to be dead.

The enemy soldiers aim 15 minutes of continuous fire at them and then, presuming them dead, start climbing down to the third sangar, which is further down the slope. This is when Sanjay Kumar and his mates make a superhuman effort. Despite their injuries, they storm the next sangar. They find it deserted except for dead bodies and unused ammunition. They turn the enemy's machinegun at the fleeing soldiers and shoot them in cold blood before they can reach the safety of the third bunker.

When they take final stock of the captured area, they find 15 bodies of Pakistani soldiers, a large cache of arms and ammunition, snow huts and tents. They sit down, bleeding from their injuries, using their first-aid kits, waiting for help to reach them. By 5.30 pm, the unit doctor reaches the bunkers. He gives the men painkillers and first aid. The rest of the team helps the injured to climb down to the base since the heights are too dangerous for stretchers to be used.

It takes Sanjay Kumar the entire night to hobble down. It is 9.30 a.m. when he reaches the Mushkoh valley from where an ambulance takes him to the field hospital at Ghumri. There are still five bullets lodged in his body; miraculously, none of them has touched his bones or vital organs. What amazes the doctors even more is that he is conscious and walking despite the unbearable pain and blood loss. After the bullets are taken out and his wounds stitched up, a helicopter shifts him to the military hospital at Srinagar. The nurse on duty is surprised that despite being bone tired he will not close his eyes. He doesn't tell her that he has seen his friends shot and dying in front of his eyes. He has killed men he never knew. He has pulled out burning guns with his hands. He has walked with bullets lodged in his body. He has suffered a degree of pain that will haunt him for life. He has scars that will remind him of a war fought on a cold, craggy ridge where mere mortals went beyond the natural instinct for self-preservation to fulfil their duty towards their country.

It takes him some time to accept that after more than a month of dodging death on a freezing mountain, his life is not at risk, he has no enemy to vanquish, his mind is without fear. He lets his mind take him to his old parents who live in the small Bhakhra-water encircled village of Bakain in Himachal Pradesh, where he ran across the green fields as a little boy. Under the influence of a heavy sedative and painkillers, he finally closes his eyes to the horrors of war and drifts off to sleep.

Sanjay Kumar was born on 3 March 1976 in Bakaingaon near Bilaspur, Himachal Pradesh, a small village with a population of 650, where the forces are a popular career choice. He was the youngest in his family, born after three sisters and two brothers. His father was a farmer who managed to make just enough to feed and clothe his family and send his children to school.

Sanjay started going to the Kalol High School, about a kilometre from his village, when he was in class one and continued to go there till he had completed his tenth standard. Since his elder brother was in the ITBP and his father's brother in the Army, Sanjay also wanted to join the armed forces. In 1994, after completing class 10, he went to Delhi to learn to drive a taxi. For some time, he earned money driving taxis but he also kept checking for Army recruitment drives. In January 1996, he got selected at a recruitment rally in Jabalpur and was enrolled in the Army as a soldier and sent to 13 JAK Rif. Sanjay Kumar's regiment had completed its CI Ops (counter-insurgency operations) tenure in Sopore, Kashmir, and was on its way to Shahjahanpur when the war broke out with Kargil. He was amongst those sent to fight in Dras and the Mushkoh valley.

'Sometimes, the afternoon when we attacked the enemy sangar flashes before my eyes and my skin breaks out into goosebumps. But most days, I don't think about it. There was nothing special about me. I was like any other boy who grew up in a village. I was never brave till I joined the Army. It was my training that gave me the courage to do what I did. Any other soldier in my place would have done the same,' says Sanjay, closing the last in a series of interviews with polite finality.

I have already made him late for lunch and he will have to hurry since he cannot reach his afternoon duties late. 'Ab mujhe jana hoga, jawan mera intezaar kar rahe honge,' (I will have to leave, the soldiers must be waiting for me) he says apologetically. He doesn't wait to hear my 'thank you'.

Based on conversations with Hav Sanjay Kumar, PVC.

Vikram Batra

It takes a one-and-half-hour flight out of Delhi and then as much time by road to drive from Kangra airport to Bandla Gaon in Palampur, Himachal Pradesh. The snow-covered Dhauladhar ranges appear and disappear at bends in the winding road and dazzle you with their magnificence. And the fragrant white roses that dot the airport and make the tourists gasp in pleasure follow you all the way to Vikram Batra Bhawan, where the late Captain Vikram Batra's old parents stay in a bright-yellow-walled bungalow. There, they stop and bloom outside the room where an oil portrait of Capt. Batra hangs on a wall. His father sits before it, draped in a pashmina shawl, asking his wife to get you a hot cup of tea, or lay the table for lunch or just corroborate what he is saying from the confines of her bedroom where she is reading the local newspaper.

On the narrow, meandering path that crosses lush green tea gardens on one side and lazy market-places on the other it is not difficult to get directions to the Param Vir Chakra (PVC) awardee's house. All you have to do is mention his name and young boys with wispy moustaches, old men with doddering gait, spectacled tailors with scissors in their hands and schoolgirls with red-ribboned plaits happily guide you with words and gestures of the hand. You don't really need the address that the gravelly voice of Mr Girdhari Lal Batra, Vikram's father, has painstakingly spelled out for you a day ago.

Not very many years back, a little boy with a puff in his hair and a twinkle in his eye roamed these very walkways, often alongside his identical twin. Luv and Kush. That was what their mother called them. They didn't have a television set at home and would slip their feet into their rubber slippers so they could sneak out of their house to Nisha Didi's next door so they could watch the TV serial *Param Vir Chakra* which aired on Sunday mornings at 10 a.m. The twins would be shiny- eyed and open-mouthed marvelling at the bravery of the men who had been awarded free India's highest gallantry medal. Afterwards, lost in conversation about just how brave the heroes in uniform had been and just how awesome the PVC was, they would walk back home.

One of the twins would actually hold the medal in his hand one day. The other wouldn't, but he would be the one responsible for getting it home—this boy was the feistier of the twins. His name was Luv. The same Luv, whose house a writer would come looking for nearly three decades later. By then he would have become Capt. Vikram Batra, the 24-year-old soldier who fought for his country on the rocky mountains of Kashmir and died trying to save another soldier.

When she was blessed with twins after the birth of two daughters, Kamal Kanta would wonder sometimes why she had been given two sons when she had asked for just one. 'Now I know. One of them was meant for the country and one for us,' she would later say. All she has of Vikram are portraits and pictures and medals and memories that she is happy to share.

She remembers the day a colleague at the school where she used to teach had told her that she had spotted Vikram at the hospital. Panicking, she had rushed there to find him with a few cuts and bruises on his body, smiling broadly. He had jumped out of the moving school bus when the door had opened suddenly at a steep turn and a little girl had lost her balance and fallen off. When his upset mother had asked him why he had been so foolhardy, he had told her he was worried that the girl would come under another bus.

Right from his childhood, Vikram was bold and fearless and always ready to help a person in need. Another time, he ran from pillar to post trying to get a gas cylinder for a new teacher in the school. The teacher had just moved to Palampur and asked for Vikram's help when he had just not been able to manage one despite all efforts. Vikram promised him that he would get him a cylinder by evening and had kept his word, carting it all the way to the teacher's house in an auto-rickshaw from the market.

In addition to his gregarious nature—he had a vast circle of friends—his inclination to help any and everyone and his happy temperament, Vikram was brilliant at studies and a national-level table tennis player. He was judged the best NCC Air Wing cadet for North Zone. He had even received a call letter from the merchant navy, and got all his uniforms stitched, but at the last moment decided not to join, telling his beleaguered father that his dream was to become an Army officer.

He took admission in Chandigarh, prepared for the combined defence services exam and got through just as he had promised his parents. The Batras went for his passing-out parade. They were thrilled to see their handsome son in uniform and wondered just how high he would go. They didn't know then that a few years later, the then Chief of Army Staff, General Ved Prakash Malik would sit in their house and tell them that if Vikram had not been martyred in Kargil, he would have been sitting in his office one day. It would make Mr Batra's chest fill with pride in spite of the tears threatening to spill over.

––––––

Yeh dil mange more!

13 Jammu and Kashmir Rifles (JAK Rif.) had completed its Kashmir tenure and the advance party had reached Shahjahanpur, its new location, when it was recalled because war had broken out. After crossing the Zoji La Pass and halting at Ghumri for acclimatization, it was placed under 56 Brigade and asked to reach Dras to be the reserve of 56 Brigade for the capture of Tololing. 18 Grenadiers had tried to get Tololing in the initial days of the conflict but had

suffered heavy casualties. Eventually, 2 Rajputana Rifles had got Tololing back.

After the capture, the men of 13 JAK Rif. walked for 12 hours from Dras to reach Tololing where Alpha Company took over Tololing and a portion of the Hump Complex from 18 Grenadiers. It was at the Hump Complex that commanding officer (CO) Lieutenant Colonel Yogesh Joshi sat in the cover of massive rocks and briefed the two young officers he had tasked with the capture of Pt. 5140, the most formidable feature in the Dras sub-sector. They could see the peak right in front with enemy bunkers at the top but from that distance they could not make out the enemy strength. To Lt Vikram Batra of Delta Company and Lt Sanjeev Jamwal of Bravo Company, that didn't matter. They were raring to go.

Col Joshi had decided that these would be the two assaulting companies that would climb up under cover of darkness from different directions and dislodge the enemy. The two young officers were listening to him quietly as he spoke. Having briefed both, he asked them what the success signals of their companies would be once they had completed their tasks. Jamwal immediately replied that his success signal would be: 'Oh! Yeah, yeah, yeah!' He said that when he was in the National Defence Academy, he belonged to the Hunter Squadron, and this used to be their slogan. Lt Col Joshi then turned to Vikram and asked him what his signal would be. Vikram thought for a while and then said it would be: 'Yeh dil mange more!' (This heart wants more!)

Despite the seriousness of the task at hand, his CO could not suppress a smile and asked him why. Full of confidence and enthusiasm, Vikram replied that he would not want to stop after that one success and would be on the lookout for more bunkers to capture.

Capture of Point 5140

It was a pitch-dark night. Lt Col Yogesh Joshi was sitting at the base of the hump from where preparatory bombardment of Pt. 5140 had commenced. He was trying to make out the movement of his troops he knew would be climbing up under cover of darkness. The Indian artillery had plastered the entire feature with high explosives. For a long time, it appeared as if the mountain was on fire and Joshi hoped that the enemy on top was dead. His hopes were, however, dashed very quickly. The Pakistanis had occupied reverse slope positions when the Indian artillery was pounding them and had now returned to fire at the Indian soldiers climbing up. From time to time, Joshi would see flashes on the dark mountain. From that he would know that the enemy was firing at his men and also just where the two teams had reached.

The enemy had also started using artillery illumination at regular intervals, which lit up the entire area for about 40 seconds. This was done to spot the climbing Indian soldiers. Joshi hoped that his boys were following the standard drill, which was that everyone freezes and tries to blend into the surroundings when the area lights up like daylight. Movement would make them visible.

Suddenly, his radio set came alive and he could make out the voice of a Pakistani soldier. He was challenging Batra, whose code name Sher Shah the enemy had intercepted. 'Sher Shah, go back with your men, or else only your bodies will go down.' The radio set crackled and then he heard Batra reply, his voice pitched high in excitement: 'Wait for an hour and then we'll see who goes back alive.' At 3.30 a.m., the CO's radio set crackled again. 'Oh! Yeah, yeah, yeah!' It was Jamwal signalling that his part of the peak had been captured. Batra and his team were taking longer since they were climbing up the steeper incline.

The next one hour was to be one of the longest for Lt Col Joshi. He could hear gunfire and see the flash of gunpowder, but had no idea what was happening at Pt. 5140. Finally, at 4.35 a.m., in the cold of the darkness, his radio set beeped again and he heard the now-famous words: 'Yeh dil mange more!' It was Batra. He and his men had captured the peak and unfurled the Tricolour there. What was most amazing was that in this attack, the Indian side did not suffer a single casualty.

After coming down, Batra would call his parents on the satellite phone. For a moment, his father would stop breathing because he would just hear 'captured' and feel that he had been captured. But then the laughing soldier would clarify that he had actually captured an enemy post. He would then call his girlfriend Dimple in Chandigarh and tell her not to worry. He was fine and she should take care of herself. That was the last time he would speak to her.

Vikram's next assignment would be Pt. 4875, from where he would not come back alive but he would leave Dimple with memories she was willing to spend a lifetime with. The battalion was de-inducted from Dras to Ghumri to rest and recoup. Less than a week later, they moved to Mushkoh. This was where greater glory was in store for Vikram.

Chandigarh, 2013

Dimple is a pretty, smiling 40-year-old, who works with a Punjab State Education Board school in Chandigarh. She teaches social studies and English to the students of classes 6–10. Till 3.30 p.m., she is busy with the children, taking classes, checking test papers, planning the next day's lessons. She has no time to even take a phone call. But after she gets back home and sits down with a cup of tea, she confesses that in the past 14 years, not a day has passed when she has not thought of Vikram.

Chandigarh is full of his memories for her, she says. 'When I pass the bus stop I remember how I would drop him there so that he could catch a bus to wherever he was going; when I'm in the University I remember how I first noticed him when he came and sat between me and a guy who was trying to get uncomfortably close and subtly told me to move from there. When I'm in the Nada Saheb gurudwara I remember how he tailed me in a parikrama (circumambulation) and then called out: "Congratulations, Mrs Batra, we have completed the fourth phera (circle) and, according to your Sikh religion, we are now man and wife." When I'm near Pinjore gardens I remember how before going to Kashmir he took a blade from his wallet, cut his thumb and put a streak of blood in my parting to dispel all my insecurities about whether he would marry me or not . . .'

Dimple and Vikram were college sweethearts. They had only attended a few months of classes together at Punjab University when Vikram left to join the Indian Military Academy. They kept in touch and decided to get married. Had Vikram come back from the Kargil War that was the plan. Only he didn't. Instead, Dimple got a phone call from a friend saying Vikram had suffered a terrible injury and she should call his parents. When she rushed to Palampur, she saw a coffin bearing his body, surrounded by a crowd of media and local people. More than 25,000 had collected for his funeral, not just from Palampur, but also from the nearby towns of Baijnath, Paprola and Nagrota.

'I didn't go closer because there was too much media there and I didn't want to break down and create a scene.' She watched quietly from a distance holding her brother's hand. Vikram's parents noticed the girl in salwar-kameez standing in the crowd but they were too upset to find out who she was.

Dimple returned to Chandigarh and decided she would rather live with his memories than get married to someone else. 'He was a wonderful, fun-loving guy. He was very handsome. He loved to do things for people, but why I miss his so much is because he was my best friend. I could tell him my innermost feelings and he would understand,' she says.

Sometimes when she accidentally looks at the clock and it shows 7.30 p.m. on a Wednesday, or on a Sunday, Dimple's heart still misses a beat. For nearly four years, till he went to war from where he did not return, that was the scheduled time for Vikram to call her without fail, irrespective of where he was. 'He could be in Palampur, Dehradun, Sopore or Delhi but the call would come and I would always stay around the phone so that I could pick it up before my father did,' she remembers with a wistful smile.

The telephone no longer rings for her at that allotted time and, even if it does, that familiar voice is no longer there. He would have called but they don't have telephone connectivity where he has gone now.

The Last Victory
7 July 1999

The wind was like a knife—cold and sharp—and Capt. Vikram Batra, who had been promoted after his first assault in June, knew it could slice the skin right off his cheekbones. To an extent, it already had.

That was why he and his 25 men from Delta Company, 13 JAK Rif., blended in so well with the barren landscape. Their grey, sunburnt faces with unkempt beards and tissue peeling off under the wind's painful whipping merged perfectly with the massive boulders behind which they were taking cover. Pt. 4875 was still 70 metres away and their task had been to reach that ridge, storm the enemy and occupy the post before daylight. Unfortunately, the evacuation of Capt. Navin, who had a badly injured leg, had taken time and it was already first light. Through the night the men had been climbing the slope with machinegun fire coming almost incessantly from the top of the ridge. Intermittently, their faces would glow in the red light of the Bofors fire that was giving them cover from the base of the Mushkoh valley.

The morning of 7 July there was a lot of pressure to proceed. Lt Col Joshi spoke to Batra at 5.30 a.m. and asked him to reconnoitre the area with Subedar Raghunath Singh. Just before the point was a narrow ledge where the enemy soldiers were and it was almost impossible to go ahead. There was no way from the left or right either and, on the spur of the moment, Batra decided that even though it was daylight he and his boys would storm the post in a direct assauLt Setting aside all concerns for personal safety, he assaulted the ledge catching the enemy unawares but they soon opened fire. Though injured, Vikram continued his charge, with supporting fire from the rest of the patrol and reached the mouth of the ledge, giving the Indian Army a foothold on the ledge. This was when he realized that one of his men had been shot.

Even as he tried to keep his chin down with a shot whistling over his head, his eyes rested on the young soldier who had been hit and was lying in a pool of blood just a few feet away. Till a short while ago he had been crying out in pain. Now he was silent.

His eyes met those of Sub Raghunath Singh, who was sitting behind a nearby boulder, maintaining an iron grip on his AK-47. 'Aap aur main usko evacuate karenge,' (We will evacuate him, you and I) Batra shouted above the din of the flying bullets.

Raghunath Sahib's experience told him that the chances of the boy being alive were slim and they shouldn't be risking their own lives trying to get him from under enemy fire.

But Batra was unwilling to leave his man. 'Darte hain,

Sahib?' (Are you afraid, sir?) he taunted the JCO.

'Darta nahin hun, Sahib,' (I am not afraid, Sir) Raghunath replied and got up.

Just as he was about to step into the open, Batra caught him by the collar: 'You have a family and children to go back to, I'm not even married. Main sar ki taraf rahunga aur aap paanv uthayenge,' (I will take the head and you take his feet) he said pushing the JCO back and taking his place instead. The moment Batra bent to pick up the injured soldier's head, a sniper shot him in the chest.

The man who had survived so many bullets, killed men in hand-to-hand combat and cleared bunkers of Pakistani intruders, fearlessly putting his own life at stake so many times, was destined to die from this freak shot.

When he was in Sopore some time earlier, Batra had had a miraculous escape when a militant's bullet had grazed his shoulder and hit the man behind him killing him on the spot. He was surprised then. As he lay dying, destiny surprised him yet again. He had plans to follow, he had tasks to achieve, an enemy to vanquish. He was surprised that the bullet had found its mark despite all those unfulfilled duties. Batra gasped in disbelief and collapsed next to the young soldier he had wanted to give a dignified death to. The blood drained out of his body even as his stunned men watched in horror.

Spurred by Batra's extreme courage and sacrifice, a squad of 10 of his men (each carrying one AK-47 rifle, six magazines and two No. 36 hand grenades) attacked through the ledge, found the Pakistanis making halwa and killed each of the enemy soldiers on top, with zero casualties of their own in that assauLt The fierceness of their attack frightened the Pakistani soldiers so much that many of them ran to the edge and jumped off the cliff, meeting a painful end in the craggy valley.

Even in his death, Vikram Batra had kept the promise he had made to a friend casually over a cup of tea at Neugal Café in Palampur, on his last visit home. When his friend had cautioned him to be careful in the war, Batra had replied: 'Either, I will hoist the Tricolour in victory or I'll come back wrapped in it.'

A tribute by Vishal Batra

If I begin with our journey, it started in a small town, Palampur, in the Dhauladhar ranges in district Kangra.

Luv, as we called Capt Vikram Batra, PVC (Posthumous), and I, Kush, his identical twin (just 14 minutes younger) had a life full of laughter and pranks till we grew up and decided that we wanted to be part of the Indian armed forces.

How fast time flies. And how all of us don't get what we want. Luv made it into the Indian Military Academy in March 1996 and I, rejected thrice by the Service Selection Board, had to settle for a career in management.

When Vikram visited us during his annual leave, looking tall and handsome in his uniform, I realized how much passion I still had for the forces. With great pride in my eyes I watched my brother marching ahead in life so much faster than we had thought.

Having got commissioned into 13 JAK Rifles with his first posting in Sopore, Vikram already had some daring face-to-face combat with the enemy in insurgency operations. We knew he was born to fight against the odds.

It was around the same time that the Kargil War happened and he was asked to move there to help fellow soldiers flush out Pakistani intruders who had entered Indian terrain. The last call Vikram made to Mom and Dad on his movement had given us some jitters, but we always knew that he was a daring officer for whom facing any challenge was a cakewalk. His last statement to one of our friends before proceeding to Kargil that either he would hoist the Tricolour or come back wrapped in it still echoes in our hearts. It showed what iron he was made of.

It's been 15 years. A lot has changed and a lot has remained the same. I have many more grey strands in my hair. Vikram remains as youthful as ever. Time cannot touch him. In these 15 years, there has hardly been any day when Vikram has not been spoken about.

The greatest memory etched in my heart so deep is from way back in 1985 when the Doordarshan-telecast serial *Param Vir Chakra*. We didn't have a TV then and would watch at our neighbours' house. I could never have imagined even in my wildest dreams that the stories we saw in this popular serial would one day become so real for us. Or that Vikram would be the hero. The famous radioed message, from a height of 18,000 feet, 'Yeh Dil maange more', by Vikram caught the fancy of millions of Indians, and they still haven't forgotten it. Or him.

So many times strangers come up to me and tell me that I look like Vikram or ask if they have seen me somewhere. I have been asked by hundreds of people if I am related to

Vikram. Each time, I know they are thinking of Vikram and I feel proud of being his brother.

Death is the ultimate truth of life but how many of us have the courage to face death with open arms? My brother Vikram was a Param Vir—Bravest of the Brave.

I salute all those soldiers who are the real Virs of this nation.

Acknowledgements

I would like to extend my sincerest thanks to Hony (Retd) Capt Bana Singh, PVC, Sub Yogender Singh Yadav, PVC, and Hav Sanjay Kumar, PVC, for sharing with me their brave stories with a humility that touched me to the core. I would also like to thank all those soldiers who shared with me their recollections of the painful wars they fought and the brave colleagues they lost. Also, the loved ones of dead heroes who welcomed me into their homes and let me sift through their albums and memories to help me know these PVCs better.

I am particularly thankful to Lt Gen (Retd) S.N. Sharma, PVSM, AVSM, brother of the late Maj Somnath Sharma, India's first PVC; Subedar (Retd) Kala Singh, who had served with both the late Lance Naik Karam Singh, PVC, and the late Sub Joginder Singh, PVC; Mrs Rajeshwari Rane, widow of the late Maj Rama Raghoba Rane, PVC, Col J.P. Chopra, VrC, who was with Maj Rane in the 1947 War; Lt Aditya Tanwar and Hav R.D. Tiwari of 4 Guards for spending a precious Saturday evening and Sunday morning helping me research Naik Yadunath Singh in their Regimental

Archives at Beas, 4 Guards for their hospitality and Number 1 guest room, and Brig (Retd) N. Bahri for passing on regimental lore about Yadunath; Maj Gen (Retd) R.P. Singh, AVSM, VSM, for permission to use material from his book on the late Maj Gurbachan Singh Salaria, PVC; Poonam Thapa, daughter of the late Lt Col Dhan Singh Thapa, PVC, for her time and memories; Hon Capt (Retd) Ram Chander and Hav (Retd) Nihal Singh, Sena Medal, of 13 Kumaon for their vivid recollections of the Battle of Rezang La; the late Hav Abdul Hamid, PVC's grandson Mr Jameel for sharing stories no one else knew; Mrs Zarine Mahir Boyce, daughter of the late Col Adi Tarapore, PVC, for her memories of her father, Col Bal Singh, Commandant, Poona Horse, for reading the draft on Col Tarapore, Lt Gen (Retd) Ajai Singh for his conversation about the 1965 War; Col (Retd) O.P. Kohli for his recollections of late Lance Naik Albert Ekka, PVC, and the BangladeshWar; Air Cmde (Retd) Ramesh V. Phadke for helping me know Flying Officer Nirmal Jit Singh Sekhon, PVC, better; the late Mrs Maheshwari Khetarpal, for her time (she passed away shortly after I spent a morning with her remembering 2/Lt Arun Khetarpal PVC), Mr Mukesh Khetarpal (Arun's brother), who told me stories about his brother with a lot of love, Risaldar Maj (Retd) Nathu Singh for war narratives (he was with Arun in his dying moments); Col (Retd) S.S. Cheema, SM, and Col S.S. Punia, who fought the 1971 War along with late Col Hoshiar Singh, PVC, for helping me reconstruct the battle and specially to Col Cheema for editing the chapters on Col Tarapore and Col Hoshiar Singh; Col Vijay Kumar, CO, 8 Mahar, and Subedar (Retd) Dilip Maske for helping me understand the bravery of late Major Ramaswamy Parameswaran, PVC; Mrs Mohini Pande, Param Vir Chakra awardee late Captain Manoj Pande's mother for sharing with me her memories of his growing years, that made her cry so many times; Brig Asthana for telling me about Manoj's tenure in the battalion; Mr Girdharilal Batra and Mrs Kamal Kanta Batra, parents of late Capt Vikram Batra, PVC, for their time and the loving lunch they gave me in their beautiful house in Bandla Gaon, Himachal Pradesh, Vikram's twin brother Vishal for his help and his friend Dimple for her memories of him.

I am also grateful to the Commanding Officers/ Commandants of all the PVC paltans for giving me access to documents, citations and war diaries, and for introducing me to retired soldiers and families of the dead heroes. The stories I wrote were based on their recollections.

Thanks also to Maj Gen (Retd) Ian Cardozo, whose book *Param Vir, Our Heroes in Battle* was a source of constant guidance and to Squadron Leader (Retd) Rana Chinna, Secretary, United Service Institution of India Centre for Armed Forces Historical Research, for giving me access to the exhaustive USI library and personally helping me find relevant war journals and books for my stories.

A sincere thank you to the Additional Directorate General of Public Information, (ADG PI), Indian Army, for providing valuable material, contact details and assistance in the project. They were a part of this book from start to finish. Thanks also to artist Rishi Kumar for stretching his work schedule to come up with face illustrations of the 21 PVCs at a very short notice.

I am particularly grateful to Col Sudhir Thakur, from 3 Engineer Regiment, for seeing this book through from start to finish with unflinching patience and for clearing every road block I encountered. Believe me, there were plenty! Sudhir was there at every step. Without him, this book couldn't have been possible. I would also like to thank Maj Gen (Retd) N.R.K. Babu, who inspired me to keep writing, right from when I joined the regiment as a young Army wife and was a little upset about having to leave behind a career in journalism, by tasking me to write the 3 Regiment history to this project where he set the ball rolling by a personal visit when it looked like permissions for the book would not come from the Army. But then we are all from 3 Engineer Regiment, which makes them family and I tend to take them for granted.

Thanks also to Brigadier and Mrs M.K. Ajith Kumar, my adopted family, for facilitating interviews in Punjab for the stories on the late Lance Naik Karam Singh PVC and the late Subedar Joginder Singh PVC and for letting me live in their Bhatinda house, feeding me and tolerating me while I worked on their personal computer almost through the night. And to their golden retriever Toffee for licking me awake when I fell asleep at the computer.

I am also grateful to Col Rajeev Singh for finding me coveted phone numbers despite the constraints of a busy command, and Whatsapping them across with a cheerful message: Ma'am I'm faster than Google. And to my ever-smiling, wise cousin Tanu whose advice, time, house, car and driver were always at my disposal.

A grateful thanks to my old friend and former *Financial Express* colleague Renu Agal for introducing me to Penguin while I was living in back-of-beyond Ferozepur, the last town on the Indo-Pak border. Thanks also to my book editor at

Penguin Anish Chandy for giving me this opportunity to give back to the Army something in return for all that it has given me. And to Archana Shankar at Random House for meticulously reading and rereading the proofs and for her patience and belief in me.

Thanks also to Manoj, my husband, for babysitting our son Saransh while I was away on my voyages of discovery and for being there to pick me up from airports and railway stations with a reassuring smile on his face. And to Saransh, for ensuring I complete the book in those moments of self-doubt: 'But Mamma, I've told all my friends. You have to do it now. Nahi toh meri beizzati ho jayegi,' he said. To my brother Col Sameer Singh Bisht, SM, for using his personal experience in Kargil for editing my Kargil drafts. And lastly to my dad Brigadier (Retd) B.S. Bisht, SM, VSM, for driving me to tears with those dreaded daily phone calls, gruffly demanding 'How many chapters have you done?' but always, always ending each conversation with an 'All the best beta'—something he has been wishing me all my life. I like to believe it works.